Palgrave Macmillan Studies in Banking and Financial Institutions

Series Editor
Philip Molyneux
University of Sharjah
Sharjah, UAE

"This book offers an overview of the funding strategies adopted over the last decade by European banks, with a focus on Italian banks. The empirical investigation of the funding carried out via bank bond issuances reveals an increase in the cost of funding faced by banks upon the introduction of the Bank Recovery and Resolution Directive (BRRD). Crespi and Mascia provide an important contribution to the current debate and enrich the literature on the interplay between regulation and bank management."

—Elena Beccalli, *Università Cattolica del Sacro Cuore, Italy*

The Palgrave Macmillan Studies in Banking and Financial Institutions series is international in orientation and includes studies of banking systems in particular countries or regions as well as contemporary themes such as Islamic Banking, Financial Exclusion, Mergers and Acquisitions, Risk Management, and IT in Banking. The books focus on research and practice and include up to date and innovative studies that cover issues which impact banking systems globally.

More information about this series at
http://www.palgrave.com/series/14678

Fabrizio Crespi · Danilo V. Mascia

Bank Funding Strategies

The Use of Bonds and the Bail-in Effect

palgrave
macmillan

Fabrizio Crespi
Department of Economics and Business
University of Cagliari
Cagliari, Italy

Danilo V. Mascia
Department of Economics and Business
University of Cagliari
Cagliari, Italy

Palgrave Macmillan Studies in Banking and Financial Institutions
ISBN 978-3-319-69412-2 ISBN 978-3-319-69413-9 (eBook)
https://doi.org/10.1007/978-3-319-69413-9

Library of Congress Control Number: 2017956909

Cover illustration: Pattern adapted from an Indian cotton print produced in the 19th century

Printed on acid-free paper

This Palgrave Macmillan imprint is published by Springer Nature
The registered company is Springer International Publishing AG
The registered company address is: Gewerbestrasse 11, 6330 Cham, Switzerland

The pizza delivery man comes to Yogi Berra after the game and says:
"Yogi, how do you want this pizza cut, into quarters or eighths?"
And Yogi says:
"Cut it in eight pieces. I'm feeling hungry tonight."

Merton Miller
(describing the MM propositions in an interview)

Preface

The liability management represents a crucial activity for banks. Due to the intrinsic maturity mismatch that characterizes their balance sheets, banks need to carefully consider different options regarding the amount and composition of the funding (e.g. more equity or more debt), the target depositor (retail or wholesale), the ideal instruments to be used (deposits, bonds, equity instruments). Moreover, the funding strategies have to be in line with the asset side profile (risk and maturity) and the legislative provisions imposed to financial intermediaries.

Yet, notwithstanding its importance, not too much literature appears to have covered the topic, at least until the blast of the financial crisis. In particular, only few academic studies have investigated, so far, the role of bonds in the funding mix of European banks; while some aggregate analyses have been proposed by the ECB and the IFM.

In this monograph, we aim to illustrate the general evolution of European banks' funding strategies during the last 10 years and to give a special focus on the importance of bonds as a funding choice for the Italian banking sector (especially after the introduction of the Bank Recovery and Resolution Directive, BRRD). Such a choice was driven by two major reasoning.

On the one hand, last decade has been a period characterized by an unprecedented recession that followed the global financial crisis and the Euro area sovereign debt crisis, as well as by the implementation of important regulatory reforms for banks (in particular, the Basel III framework and the BRRD). As demonstrated by the ECB, economic and financial conditions after the crisis have strongly influenced the behaviour of European banks with regards to funding.

The focus on the Italian bank bonds market, on the other hand, lies in the fact that, historically, Italian banks (much more than their European peers) have placed to retail investors huge amounts of bonds (as if they were a sort of surrogate for deposits), and have strongly used this funding instrument at least until 2012. Moreover, given the structure of the financial system (traditionally bank-oriented) and the transformation occurred in the last few years (including more than one case of *bail-out*), it is not inappropriate to say that the examination of Italian banks' funding strategies represents an interesting case study.

Furthermore, our spotlight on the Italian market is motivated by the interest to observe whether the recent implementation of the BRRD has somehow affected the issuances of new bonds by Italian banks and the related cost of funding. Notably, we believe that Italy represents a good laboratory for our analysis, provided that the Italian Resolution Authority credibly implemented a so-called *burden-sharing* operation for four banks just some weeks before the full implementation of the BRRD. The monograph, therefore, is structured as follows.

In Chap. 1, we provide a deep review of the literature regarding banks' funding strategies and, in particular, we investigate how the funding strategies carried out in Europe have changed over the last ten years. The analysis is accompanied by the presentation of some aggregated statistics—drawn from the European Central Bank statistical database—regarding the funding mix of credit institutions operating in the major Euro zone countries.

Chapter 2, instead, offers a focus about the funding strategies of Italian banks with a particular emphasis on bonds and their importance on Italian households' financial wealth. Here again, we support our analysis through the use of some aggregated statistics—drawn from the Bank of Italy statistical database—regarding the Italian banking sector.

In Chap. 3, we analyse the characteristics of the main bonds' categories issued by Italian banks. Using a sample of data extrapolated by a specialized platform ('eXact 4 Suite' by Analysis) we can appreciate the number of issuing institutions, the amount of bonds issued, and other key aspects of the outstanding bonds in the Italian market.

Finally, Chap. 4 concludes this book by providing an analysis of the effects that the implementation of the BRRD has generated on the yields (at issuance) offered by bank bonds and, consequently, on the cost of funding borne by banks. We carry out this analysis by employing a unique set of hand-collected data. Furthermore, we illustrate a few very recent case studies highlighting the impact of the BRRD on some problematic banks in Italy (eventually ending up either with resolution, liquidation or precautionary recapitalization) and the severe effects that these phenomena have generated on retail bondholders.

Cagliari, Italy

Fabrizio Crespi
Danilo V. Mascia

Acknowledgements

We would like to thank two anonymous reviewers for their helpful comments. Furthermore, we are thankful to Philip Molyneux, series editor for Studies in Banking and Financial Institutions, for the opportunity to publish this volume, and to the staff at Palgrave Macmillan, especially Aimee Dibbens and Tula Weis, for helpful guidance.

Cagliari, Italy
August 2017

Fabrizio Crespi
Danilo V. Mascia

Contents

1 The Funding Strategies of European Banks: A Discussion 1

1.1 Introduction 2

1.2 Bank Funding Strategies: Literature Review and Main Topics 4

1.3 The Funding Structures of European Banks: Evidence from Aggregated Data 27

1.4 Conclusions 46

References 46

2 The Funding Strategies of Italian Banks: The Importance of Bonds 49

2.1 Introduction 50

2.2 The Italian Banking System: An Overview 51

2.3 The Funding Strategies of Italian Banks: Evidence from Aggregated Data 56

2.4 Households Investments in Banks' Bonds: A Changed Game 61

2.5 Conclusions 66

References 67

3 **The Different Types of Bonds Issued by Italian Banks: An Overview** 69
3.1 Introduction 70
3.2 Rules and Legislation Governing Banks' Bonds Issuance: A Short Summary 71
3.3 The Main Features of Italian Bank Bonds: Evidence from a Comprehensive Database 80
3.4 The Characteristics of Bonds: Some Examples 86
3.5 Conclusions 90
References 91

4 **The Bail-in Effect: How the Cost of Funding Through Bonds has Changed After the Introduction of the BRRD** 93
4.1 Introduction 94
4.2 The BRRD 95
4.3 The Bail-in Tool 98
4.4 The Effect of *Bail-in* on the Cost of Funding Through Bonds of Italian Banks: An Empirical Analysis 100
4.5 The New Approach to Bank Resolution After the Introduction of the BRRD—*Case Studies* 108
4.6 Conclusions 113
References 114

Conclusions 117

Appendices A1 and A2 119

References 143

Index 145

About the Authors

Fabrizio Crespi is a Researcher at the University of Cagliari and a Contract Professor at ALTIS (the Postgraduate School Business & Society of the Catholic University of the Sacred Heart of Milan). After completing a PhD in "The economics of institutions and business systems", he has focused his academic career on financial innovation. His main research concerns asset-backed securitization, asset management products, asset allocation and financial planning, and innovative portfolio strategies.

Danilo V. Mascia is a Research Fellow at the University of Cagliari (Italy) and a former Visiting Academic Research Fellow at Leeds University Business School (UK). After gaining his BSc and MSc in Economics in Sardinia, he moved to the University of Amsterdam, where he was awarded the title of MSc in Business Economics. He later received his PhD in Business Economics from the University of Cagliari, together with the title of *Doctor Europaeus*. His research interests are in the areas of banking, regulation, and financing of small and medium firms.

List of Figures

Fig. 1.1	Developments in funding of MFIs	21
Fig. 1.2	Debt securities as % of total assets, selected countries	36
Fig. 1.3	Deposits as percentage of total assets, selected countries	36
Fig. 1.4	Loan-to-deposit ratio, selected countries	43
Fig. 2.1	Items contributing to the decrease of ROE between years 2006–2007 and 2015–2016 (percentage points)	56
Fig. 2.2	Loans-to-deposits ratio of Italian banks; January 1999–June 2017	59
Fig. 2.3	Breakdown of banks' debt, by main balance sheet categories; January 1999–June 2017	60
Fig. 2.4	Bonds over liabilities; January 1999–June 2017	61
Fig. 2.5	Capital and reserves over total assets; January 1999–June 2017	61
Fig. 2.6	Changing composition of households' wealth (flow view)	64

List of Tables

Table 1.1	Number of credit institutions (data at the beginning of the year)	30
Table 1.2	Debt securities issued (outstanding amounts at the end of the period, in millions of Euro)	31
Table 1.3	Debt securities issued (as % of total assets)	34
Table 1.4	Deposit liabilities (outstanding amounts at the end of the period, in millions of Euro)	37
Table 1.5	Deposit funding ratio (i.e. Deposits over Total Assets)	39
Table 1.6	Loan to deposit ratio	41
Table 1.7	Loans to total assets	44
Table 2.1	Italian household financial wealth composition (millions of Euro and percentages)	62
Table 3.1	Listing of bonds vs seniority and type	84
Table 3.2	Seniority vs type of bond	85
Table 3.3	Return vs type of bond and seniority	85
Table 4.1	List of banks and related positions in the country ranking	101
Table 4.2	Summary statistics	105

Table A1 Data gathered from the statistical database ("Base Dati Statistica", BDS), available at Bank of Italy, along with authors' calculations 120
Table A2 Sampled banks listed according to the number of bond issuances; data gathered from "eXact 4 Suite" 127

1

The Funding Strategies of European Banks: A Discussion

Abstract The financial turmoil occurred during the last decade has heavily affected the stability of the financial systems and the European economy. Indeed, the implications generated by the crises on the real economy, along with the important regulatory changes affecting banks, have surely had an impact on the behaviour of European banks in regards to their approach towards funding. The analysis of aggregated data for the last ten years confirms the widespread view in the literature that, at least for the largest European economies, retail deposits have acquired an increasing importance in terms of main funding instrument available to the credit institutions. Indeed, banks have progressively replaced wholesale funding in favour of deposits. Moreover, our analysis highlights a decline in the volume of bonds issued by the financial institutions over the last few years.

Keywords Funding strategies · Retail deposits · Wholesale funding
Bonds

F. Crespi and D. V. Mascia, *Bank Funding Strategies*, Palgrave Macmillan Studies in Banking and Financial Institutions, https://doi.org/10.1007/978-3-319-69413-9_1

1.1 Introduction

It is well known that the traditional banking business (commercial banking) mainly consists in the activity of collecting deposits and granting credits. Due to the fact that the average maturity of deposits is normally shorter than the average maturity of credits (so-called, maturity mismatch), banks are subject to an array of typical risks such as credit risk, interest rate risk, as well as funding and liquidity risk.

In particular, banks are vulnerable to liquidity and funding risk due to their structural role in the maturity transformation of short-term deposits into long-term loans. The liquidity risk refers to the ability of a bank to fund assets and meet obligations as they come due, without incurring unacceptable losses. Liquidity can be achieved by banks in different ways: by using (free or minimum) reserves, or the standing facilities and open market operations granted by a country's Central Bank, by exploiting the interbank market, by selling assets via securitization, or simply by issuing new deposits as the old ones come due. This last possibility is inherent to the funding risk, which is the risk that a bank will be unable to efficiently meet expected and unexpected current and future cash flows, as well as collateral needs, without affecting daily operations or the financial condition of the bank. These risks may materialize at a specific bank or be systemic.[1]

It is then fundamental for a bank to manage the way in which financial resources are collected to fund the business. Indeed, banks have a range of possible sources of funding available to them, including savers' and investors' deposits, wholesale funding, as well as the bank's capital base. The decisions about the amount and compositions of these financial resources (debt and equity), the kind of creditor counterpart (retail

---

[1]Le Leslé (2012) reports: "*Funding and liquidity management are interrelated. Virtually every transaction has implications for a bank's funding needs and, more immediately, for its liquidity management. A bank's funding strategy will condition liquidity management needs. Hence, the risks embedded in the chosen funding strategy will translate into risks that liquidity management will have to address. Failure to properly manage funding risk may suddenly manifest itself as a liquidity problem, should those sources withdraw funding at short notice. Conversely, inadequate liquidity risk management may place unmanageable strains on a bank's funding strategy by requiring very large amounts of funding to be raised at short notice.*"

or wholesale funding), and the characteristics of the instruments used to collect deposits (maturity, fixed or variable rate, callable option, etc.) constitute what is normally called 'liability management'.[2]

Similarly to other types of companies, banks' liability management is strictly linked to the characteristics of the asset side of the balance sheet (level of credit risk, maturities, composition and volume of the banking book compared to the securities portfolio, etc.) or, more broadly, to the business model of the bank.[3] Funding should then be assessed based on a holistic balance sheet approach: the adequacy of funding should be measured alongside capital and liquid assets to determine the resiliency of bank funding, both in normal times and in times of stress. Indeed, the term 'asset and liability management' contains the global strategy used by a bank to manage the total composition and risk of its business, thus to maintain a durable financial stability over time.

Another important constraint in the liability management process is the incidence of regulation: the Basel III legislation requirements (including the Net Stable Funding Ratio, NSFR), the Total Loss-Absorbing Capacity (TLAC) rules, the introduction of the BRRD and the Bail-in legislation, all represent external constraints that will influence the future funding strategies of European banks.

The funding and the capital structure of banks are topics of interest for a number of reasons. First of all, the determinants of the banks' funding and capital structure are distinct from those of non-financial corporations, due to the fact that banks are subject to capital regulation. Given that they are largely funded by deposits, a significant share

[2]Funding strategies, or funding models/structures, are other terms often used to describe the way in which banks raise debt. Even if this book is mainly focused on a particular form of debt instrument (i.e. bonds), we use the above terms as a synonym of liability management. Capital management is the term specifically used to describe strategic decisions about the amount and composition of capital in the form of equity instruments.

[3]For example, the funding strategies of commercial banks and investment banks diverge substantially. Another factor that influences the funding strategies of banks is the structure of the financial system in which they operate: bank-oriented models, in which bank loans represent the main financial source for enterprises, and market-led models, where corporates primarily raise funds in capital markets, represent different environments for the banks' funding choices. Similarly, the size of a bank and the level of internationalization of its business produce effects on the funding strategies adopted.

of which is covered by guarantee schemes, banks are required to hold minimum amounts of capital to absorb losses and mitigate moral hazard concerns. From a macroeconomic point of view, changes in the composition and cost of bank funding have important implications for the provision of credit and, consequently, for economic output and inflation. Moreover, a vast literature demonstrates the influence of funding structures on crisis propagation mechanisms and individual bank performance.

In a microeconomic sense, bank liability and funding composition represent a valuable early warning indicator of vulnerabilities, perhaps more powerful than conventional capital ratios or than asset side indicators, such as nonperforming loans.

The aim of this chapter is to introduce the main issues regarding the bank funding strategies (with a special focus on the issuance of bonds), and to analyse how the choices of European banks have changed over time, especially after the blast of the financial crisis (2008–2009) and the Euro crisis (2011–2012). Different studies have indeed emphasized how these dramatic periods have reshaped the structure of the liabilities side of banks' balance sheets,[4] especially through the impact of the European Central Bank extraordinary monetary measures.

1.2 Bank Funding Strategies: Literature Review and Main Topics

The acquisition of financial resources through different kind of debt instruments, and from different counterparties (retail investors, other financial intermediaries, the central bank, etc.), represents the so-called liability management process. If we consider it together with the capital management (i.e. the decisions about the adequate level of capital to comply with regulatory requirements or, more generally, to reach the desired target), we can refer to the overall funding policy of a bank.

[4] See Van Rixtel and Gasperini (2013), Van Ritxtel et al. (2015).

Banks fund themselves through a wide range of financial instruments, from both retail and wholesale sources. The formers include customer deposits, predominantly from households: these deposits have normally short-term maturities, but households can also be buyers of long-term debt instruments such as bonds.[5] Wholesale funding broadly consists of funding from private markets, used to supplement customer deposits in financing bank operations. In the short term, wholesale funding includes interbank loans, with a prominent role for short-term US dollar funding and other short-term debt, most notably repurchase agreements (repos) and commercial paper (CP), as well as certificates of deposit. At longer maturities, banks issue medium-term notes (MTNs) and bonds; these long-term debt instruments, when issued on international markets, are bought by institutional investors, such as insurance companies, pension and mutual funds. In addition to deposit and wholesale funding, banks can access central bank liquidity and raise capital (basically equity).

Historically, the following have been considered the main goals of the funding policy of a bank:

- **Growth of funding**: this goal was once considered essential to increase the business of the bank. Obviously, the growth of the financial resources should be achieved at the right cost, and considering the overall level of interest rate risk and maturities mismatch that the management thinks to be adequate. In the last decade, however, many banks have reshaped their organizational structure and their business models: in Italy, for example, the period after the government debt crisis (2011–2012) has coincided with a widespread credit crunch phenomenon, during which even commercial banks have (at least partially) redirected their business to asset management and advisory services. Consequently, the growth of funding (especially through the issuance of bonds) has no more played a central role.

[5] As we will see in Chap. 2, this is the typical situation for small banks in Italy, which usually place their bonds to retail depositors.

- **Composition of funding**: the various forms of deposits are characterized by different costs and stability levels. A bank should achieve a right mix of funding sources, also considering the constraints imposed by regulation. Moreover, the composition of funding should grant a sufficient level of flexibility, that is the possibility to modify (in the short term) the forms of deposits used, thus to exploit favourable changes in interest rate conditions.
- **Stability of funding**: in this respect, deposits from households have always been considered more stable than wholesale funding, especially when protected by deposit guarantee schemes; furthermore, banks usually have a significant bargaining power to impose their conditions on households' deposits. Wholesale funding, on the other hand, boomed in the years before the crisis: especially large international banks were able to obtain short-term financial sources from wholesale financiers at low cost.[6] But a funding policy that relies too much on wholesale funding can be very dangerous, as the aftermath of the financial crisis demonstrated. Indeed, the liquidity conditions in the wholesale market can change rapidly, particularly for highly leveraged banks. It is well known that in the months after the bankruptcy of Lehmann Brothers, the liquidity provided by central banks became the major source of wholesale funding and, at the same time, governments across the globe were forced to provide support to the banking systems through a range of different measures. Moreover, wholesale funding is characterized by a greater interest rate sensitivity and, especially if unsecured, it is more influenced by the risk and reputation of the borrowing bank.

Other typical elements of the funding policy of a bank, especially referring to the relationships with retail depositors, concern the choices about the product characteristics,[7] the distribution channels, and the

[6]Before the financial crisis, short-term wholesale funding was mainly unsecured. Since 2007, the share of collateralized funding in overall wholesale bank funding has increased considerably (Agur 2013).

[7]Technical forms of retail deposits can vary substantially; apart from the difference between short-term and long-term maturities, other contractual conditions can influence the liquidity and risk

pricing mechanisms to be used. As regards the pricing, it is important to consider how much a bank can act as price maker with regard to certain types of deposits or, conversely, how much the level of competition forces the bank to accept the given set of market conditions. In fact, while in the wholesale funding market the level of efficiency can be considered high (as the cost of funding is in line with the current term structure and the estimated risk of the borrowing bank), the conditions in the retail funding market can be more opaque and overall inefficient. For example, a local bank with a high market share in a limited stretch of territory could better exploit long-term relationships with retail clients, possibly offering lower rates on deposits thus to reduce its cost of funding. However, due to the growing importance of the e-banking with the consequent possibility (also for retail clients) to access online banking services, these kinds of opportunities (yet existing) should diminish. Similarly, the increased transparency requirements introduced by MiFID II and by the Insurance Distribution Directive (IDD) should reduce the opacity of certain forms of funding instruments (such as bonds) normally issued by banks.

Academic research has since long investigated banks' funding strategies from different points of view. However, it is not inappropriate to say that the number of papers related to this topic has grown considerably due to the following events:

a. the general globalization of the financial systems, that has increased the opportunity for international banks to raise money abroad and has enlarged the wholesale interbank market;
b. the evolution of financial innovation that, through securitization and derivatives instruments, has created new models for funding the banking business[8];

---

of deposits. As we will see in Chap. 3, this is true especially for bonds, in which the range of different structures and embedded options is very large.

[8]During the last few decades, financial markets and banks became strongly interconnected. Banks improved their risk-hedging abilities through financial markets and opened new avenues of funding, such as the "originate-to-distribute" securitisation model. Moreover, the rapid growth of

c. the financial crisis, that has largely reshaped the business models of many banks around the world, and has forced central banks (and governments) to play a new and extraordinary role as lenders of last resort;
d. the continuing redefinition of the regulatory requirements to improve the overall stability of the banking systems (Basel III framework and other rules).

Considering that a review of the entire literature related to the bank funding strategies would never be exhaustive, we propose the following topics and related considerations.

1.2.1 Debt and Equity: The Determinants of Bank Capital Structure

As for other non-financial companies, a bank should decide its level of leverage, namely its optimal capital structure. Indeed, even if the traditional banking business is mainly financed through debt, the level of capital must meet the regulatory requirements and be appropriate to the risk-taking propensity of the management.

Theoretical reasoning related to the determinants of the use of debt, and the right level of leverage, is largely widespread in the corporate finance literature: starting from the Modigliani and Miller basic proposition that capital structure is irrelevant to determine the value of a non-financial firm, a long series of studies have investigated different aspects of this topic.[9] As reported in Van Rixtel et al. (2015), firm-specific determinants of long-term debt issuance include, for example, agency costs, asymmetric information and tax benefits; but also

investment banking activity, both by pure investment banks and universal banks, led to a growing reliance on wholesale funding, especially at short maturities (Van Rixtel and Gasperini 2013).

[9]Frank and Goya (2009), for instance, investigate the relative importance of 38 factors in the leverage decisions of publicly traded US firms.

macroeconomic and financial market conditions can influence debt issuance by non-financial firms.

But what about the banks' capital structure? What determines the right level of capitalization sought by the management? A first idea is that regulatory requirements could represent, *per se*, a strong constraint, so that bank managers often want to hold less capital than is required by regulatory authorities. In this case, the amount of capital is simply determined by the bank capital requirements and, consequently, the leverage ratio should be similar for all the banks complying with the same regulation.[10] Empirically, however, different studies[11] show that the levels of bank capital are much higher than the regulatory minimum, and this could be explained by banks holding capital buffers in excess of the minimum, in order not to be forced to raise equity on short notice to comply with regulatory limits (which could eventually be costly).

In a paper specifically dedicated to this topic, Gropp and Heider (2009) conversely find that there is a large variation in US and EU banks' capital ratios, and that capital requirements and buffers may only be of second order importance in determining the capital structure of most banks. The main findings of this study are the following:

- Standard cross-sectional determinants of firms' capital structures also apply to large, publicly traded banks in the US and Europe (except for banks close to the minimum capital requirements). This means that the sign and significance of the effect of most variables influencing the bank capital structure are identical to the ones found for non-financial firms.
- The observed high levels of banks' discretionary capital do not appear to be explained by buffers that banks hold to protect against the risk of falling below the minimum capital requirement.
- Unobserved time-invariant bank fixed-effects are important in explaining the variation of banks' capital structures. Banks appear

[10]This first reasoning is present in Mishkin (2000).

[11]See Berger et al. (2008).

to have stable capital structures at specific levels for each bank. Moreover, in a dynamic framework, banks' target leverage is time-invariant and bank specific. Both of these findings for banks mirror those found for non-financial firms.[12]

Another strand of the literature about the use of debt and the capital structure of banks is related to the concept of market discipline: in this respect, banks' capital structure should be the outcome of pressures emanating from shareholders, debt holders and depositors. As reported by Van Rixtel et al. (2015), different studies treat bank debt as a device to ensure market discipline that alleviates agency problems and information asymmetries (which are likely to be pronounced in the banking business). For example, in Flannery (1994) the disciplining effect is achieved through the issuance of short-term debt instruments, which are considered valuable contracting devices for banks, as changes in bank risk will be promptly reflected in funding costs. Evanoff et al. (2011) suggest that banks should be forced to issue subordinated debt, as banks' ability in doing so may be considered a market signal of their viability.

In any case, Van Rixtel et al. (2015) suggest to be careful in applying conventional corporate finance theories of agency costs and asymmetric information to the financing decisions of banks. Indeed, these theories are based on the trade-off considerations between debt and equity issuance, which are relevant for non-bank corporations, but much less so for banks. When looking at actual equity issuance data for banks, it is clear that there is no pronounced trade-off with debt issuance; even booming stock markets do not induce banks to issue great amounts of equity instead of debt.

[12]The authors also find that, in the observed period (1991–2004), banks have entirely financed their balance sheet growth via non-deposit liabilities, which implies that the composition of banks' total liabilities has shifted away from deposits. But this evidence is valid in the pre-crisis setting: as we will explain later, after 2008 the bank funding strategies have dramatically changed.

1.2.2 The Impact of Regulation: Basel III Framework and the Bail-in Regulation

Another important aspect that can (and will) influence banks' funding strategies is the increasing pressure of regulatory requirements. It is well known that the capital deficits suffered by banks during the 2007–2009 global financial crisis, and the goal to prevent taxpayers from bearing the costs of future bailouts in case of crisis, have lead to an unprecedented reinforcement of banks' loss-absorbing capacity.

Specifically, starting from 2014, the Basel III framework has dramatically increased the capital requirements for banks: in 2019, with the full implementation of Basel III,[13] the minimum CET 1 ratio (plus the capital conservation buffer) will reach 7%, and the minimum total capital ratio 10.5%. Moreover, other measures introduced by the Basel III framework could influence the capital structure and the funding choices of European banks.

The first one is the Basel III leverage ratio, which is defined as the capital measure (the numerator) divided by the exposure measure (the denominator), with this ratio expressed as a percentage.[14] A minimum requirement of 3% for the leverage ratio during the period from 1 January 2013 to 1 January 2017 has been tested, even if the measure is not yet a binding one.

Second, Basel III requires that a bank meet both short-term and longer term liquidity ratios. These ratios measure the bank's potential cash outflows against hypothetical inflows from assets considered *repossessable* or *salable*. In this respect, two measures have been introduced: the Liquidity coverage ratio (short term) and the Net stable funding ratio (long-term). To determine the Liquidity Coverage Ratio (LCR)

---

[13]Basel III was introduced in the EU by the so-called CRD IV package.

[14]The capital measure is the Tier 1 capital of the risk-based capital framework as defined in paragraphs 49–96 of the Basel III framework. The exposure measure for the leverage ratio should generally follow the accounting value, subject to the following: (i) on-balance sheet, non-derivative exposures are included in the exposure measure net of specific provisions or accounting valuation adjustments; (ii) netting of loans and deposits is not allowed. See Basel Committee on Banking Supervision (2014a), *Basel III leverage ratio framework and disclosure requirements*, for a deeper description.

the bank compares its highly liquid assets (HLAs) to its total net cash outflow (TNCO) over 30 calendar days. The TNCO represents all expected cash flows from the bank's outstanding balances (liabilities or off-balance sheet commitments) that mature within 30 days multiplied by expected runoff/drawdown rates.

The overall LCR ratio is expressed as follows:

$$\frac{\text{highly liquid assets}}{\text{total net cash outflows over the next 30 calendar days}} > 100\%$$

HLAs are assumed to be easily convertible into cash, with no substantial losses, during a 30-day time frame.[15] With this rule, the regulators' goal is to force banks in building sound balance sheets, where the difference between highly liquid assets minus total net cash outflows is higher than zero, namely the LCR ratio must be greater than 100%.

In practice, however, many banks might want a safety buffer, and could establish a target LCR measured as 100% + X%. To improve its LCR, a bank could increase the numerator (HLAs) and/or decrease the denominator (TNCO). Unfortunately, some measures that improve one side of the fraction can have detrimental effects on the other side. A way to improve the LCR is to pay back existing liabilities that mature within 30 days and purchase longer term liabilities, thus improving the TNCO. Of course, this depends on the existing counterparties' willingness to accept an early redemption of the funds and the bank's ability to acquire longer term liabilities. In any case, the aforementioned approach highlights how crucial regulatory requirements can be in forcing banks to adapt and change their funding strategies.[16]

A longer term measure, the Net Stable Funding Ratio (NSFR), requires a bank to compare assumptions about its required stable

---

[15]See Basel Committee on Banking Supervision (2014b), *Liquidity coverage ratio disclosure standards*, for more details about HLAs.

[16]Another related aspect concerns the fact that long-term unsecured bonds issued by banks are not considered HLA. This means that a bank could find more difficult to place its bonds if other banks do not want to buy them in order to comply with the LCR rules.

funding (RSF) and its available stable funding (ASF) in a one-year time horizon. The ratio is expressed as follows:

$$\frac{\text{availble amount of stable funding}}{\text{required amount of stable funding}} > 100\%$$

The ASF is the bank's current liabilities that are assumed to be available to the bank within one year. The amount of ASF is measured based on the broad characteristics of the relative stability of an institution's funding sources, including the contractual maturity of its liabilities and the differences in the propensity of different types of funding providers to withdraw their funding. The amount of ASF is calculated by first assigning the carrying value of an institution's capital and liabilities to one of five categories. The amount assigned to each category is then multiplied by an ASF factor, and the total ASF is the sum of the weighted amounts. The bank must assign its equity and liabilities to one of these categories, determine the current total amount for each category, and multiply by its corresponding ASF factor.[17]

Similarly, the amount of RSF funding is measured based on the broad characteristics of the liquidity risk profile of an institution's assets and off-balance sheet (OBS) exposures. The amount of required stable funding is calculated by first assigning the carrying value of an institution's assets to the categories indicated by the Basel III framework. The amount assigned to each category is then multiplied by its associated required stable funding (RSF) factor, and the total RSF is thus the sum of the weighted amounts added to the amount of OBS activity (or potential liquidity exposure) multiplied by its associated RSF factor.

Here again, the management of the NSFR can influence the funding choices of a bank. For example, if the bank's NSFR is too low, the average maturity of its liabilities might be too short, and this could consequently force the bank to change the composition of its funding.

[17]For more details, see Basel Committee on Banking Supervision (2014c), *Basel III: the net stable funding ratio.*

In addition to the Basel III framework, European banks must meet the requirements of the Bank Recovery and Resolution Directive (BRRD) that, starting from 2016, has introduced new rules for the resolution of distressed banks. In particular, the BRRD requires that a bank must maintain an adequate amount of *bail-inable* liabilities, thus to absorb losses in case of distress and to restore minimum capital ratios. Specifically, the regulation about the Minimum Requirement for own funds and Eligible Liabilities (MREL) has been introduced by the UE through the Commission Delegated Regulation (EU) 2016/1450 of 23 May 2016. The amount of MREL is determined by the Resolution Authority.

MREL is divided in three components: (i) the Loss Absorption Amount (LAA), which must be present in the current balance sheet; (ii) the recapitalization amount (RCA); (iii) and the Deposit Guarantee Scheme Adjustment (negative sign). In particular, LAA is the maximum between: (a) the sum of requirements under Pillar 1, Pillar 2 and the combined buffer requirement; (b) the Basel I minimum floor. But the Resolution Authority could impose a higher or lower amount. At the moment, the BRRD expresses the MREL requirement as a percentage of total liabilities and own funds; the proposed revision of the BRRD (BRRD2) could change the denominator of the ratio, opting for the use of Risk Weighted Assets (RWA).

In November 2015, the Financial Stability Board has stipulated that Global Systemically Important Banks (G-SIB) should have a Total Loss-Absorbing Capacity (or TLAC) equal to 16% of their risk weighted assets from January 2019, and equal to 18% of their RWAs starting from 2022. The instruments that can be used to meet the TLAC rules include regulatory capital requirement instruments, subordinated unsecured instruments, and senior unsecured debt.[18] G-SIB will then have to decide how to meet the TLAC requirements: these requirements, indeed, could be satisfied either with equity or *bail-inable* debt. In any

[18]At the moment, the MREL requirements and the TLCA requirements are similar but non exactly the same. The BRRD2 will probably introduce a MREL requirement for G-SIB in line with the TLCA rule, so to avoid a duplication of rules for the same bank.

case, such a choice will influence the banks' optimal level and composition of loss-absorbing liabilities. In a recent paper, Mendicino et al. (2017), try to predict the optimal size and composition of banks' total absorbing capacity: their model estimates that a very important role will be probably played by the *bail-inable* debt.

1.2.3 Financial Crises and Funding Strategies: The Impact on European Banks

The interest on banks' funding strategies has grown substantially after the blast of the global financial crisis (2007–2009); indeed, the crisis acted as a catalyst for major adjustments in banks' business and funding models. Especially for European banks, these adjustments were later reinforced by the subsequent Euro area crisis (2010–2012).

As reported by Van Rixtel and Gasperini (2013), financial crises and developments in bank funding are strongly correlated, as weaknesses on the asset side of banks' balance sheet tend to trigger funding problems. To analyse the impact of the recent crises on bank funding strategies, we will follow the results reported by different papers produced by institutional organizations such as the European Central Bank (ECB), the International Monetary fund (IMF) and the Bank for International Settlements (BIS).

One of the first analyses was provided by the ECB in May 2009 (see ECB 2009). Yet in the middle of the crisis, the ECB noted how the funding sources and strategies of a panel of banks had altered significantly. Liquidity had become a scarce good and all funding sources had gradually been affected. Deposits had been affected to a lesser extent and central bank money had remained available throughout the turmoil, as central banks stepped up their efforts to support funding needs at an early stage of the crisis.

One immediate reaction of banks that previously relied mainly on wholesale financing was to change their funding to more stable sources. Surveyed banks confirmed that deposits had become the preferred source of funding. The increased interest on deposits, however, reduced the potential market share of banks that were already reliant on retail deposits, due to an increase in competition for scarce resources.

The government and central bank measures were at that moment fundamental to avoid a full-blown collapse of the banking system; the banks, unable to issue long-term debt instruments,[19] shifted their focus to short-term funding, as they were concerned about the day-to-day market developments. Conditions in the repo market had tightened, and the range of assets as collateral had narrowed: many banks quickly understood the importance of collateral management, and increased the strategic reserves of eligible assets in order to have access to central bank funding.[20] A deleveraging process had begun, and no one could exactly estimate the period in which the markets would have restored to normal functioning.[21]

The ECB (2009) also reports another important aspect. Before the crisis, the global economy was characterized by strong economic growth, low-interest rates and risk premia, and abundant liquidity. At the same time, banks' leverage was expanding rapidly.[22] The growth of loan stocks was partly offset by the growth of deposits. However, despite the fact that deposits were increasing, the magnitude of lending surpassed that of deposits in several banks. As banks' stocks of deposits were not sufficient to provide an adequate base for their growing business, banks resorted to other available sources for funding, such as securitization, covered bonds and interbank markets.[23]

---

[19]Confidence in banks had eroded, risk aversion had increased, and investors such as money market and mutual funds had to deal with their own liquidity difficulties (redemptions). It was then very challenging for banks to issue bonds in a dried market; moreover, unsecured bonds and covered bonds had to compete with government guaranteed instruments. ECB was worried that government-guaranteed funding could crowd out bank debt for a long time.

[20]ECB extended consequently the range of eligible assets.

[21]Another immediate consequence of the financial crisis was the dramatic increase in funding costs, especially for bonds. Subsequently, the extraordinary measures of monetary policies, yet in place nowadays, drastically changed the interest rate environment, and the cost of funding for banks basically went down to zero.

[22]Banks' balance sheet expanded significantly from 2003 to 2007 (+53%) due to the availability of ample liquidity.

[23]The ECB also signalled an increased imbalance between the longer term lending to costumers and the short-term funding.

Similar considerations are expressed by Le Leslé (2012) in an IMF paper. Comparing European banks funding metrics with those of international peers, the author shows how the loan-to-deposit ratio (LDR)—which measures the extent to which customers' loans are financed by customers' deposits—, and the funding gap (i.e. the potential shortfall of customers' deposits to support customers' loans) were unfavourable for the European banks in June 2012. Typically, a low/robust LDR (below 100%) indicates that customers' loans are funded by customers' deposits, while a LDR above 100% indicates that wholesale funding is needed to complement insufficient deposits. At that time, LDRs averaged 118% in Europe (down from 140% in 2006), well above the United States (62%, down from 80%) and Japan (78%, down from 116%). European banks had the highest level of reliance on short-term wholesale funding, making them more susceptible to external shocks.

In 2012, differences between European banks and American peers also concerned the use of debt. Indeed, bank debt issuance in Europe, both senior and subordinated, towered above the amount issued by banks in the United States, Asia and emerging economies (EEs). In particular, covered bonds were (and yet are) a typical European funding vehicle, whereas US banks tend to prefer off-balance sheet securitizations. Term debt in Europe and the United States was primarily made up from senior unsecured debt (41% and 66% of total, respectively). However, Le Leslé (2012) signalled that aggregate net issuance for senior unsecured debt had turned the most negative in 15 years, which indicated how banks had replaced expensive debt funding with cheaper ECB Long-Term Refinancing Operations (LTROs).[24] This trend was exacerbated by shifting in investor preferences away from banks' unsecured debt: the author estimated that long-term investors, such as insurance companies, were likely to adjust their portfolios' composition in line with the upcoming Solvency II requirements. Therefore, bank covered bonds should increase due to their preferential capital treatment,

[24] The same indication is reported by the ECB itself in an article dedicated to the composition and cost of bank funding edited in Economic Bulletin (see ECB 2016).

while term unsecured debt (both senior and subordinated) would decline in the near future.

In April 2012 the ECB, through a new report, offered analyses about the changes in bank financing patterns (see ECB 2012). Using statistics for monetary financial institutions (MFI) domiciled in the Euro area from 1999 to the end of 2012, five categories of bank funding were investigated: interbank, customer deposits, debt securities, central bank funding and capital.

A significant trend was discovered in the interbank market: interbank liabilities as a proportion of banks' total assets fell substantially from the third quarter of 2008. This was accompanied by a rise in the share of domestic bank liabilities in total interbank liabilities, in the largest Euro area economies.[25]

With regards to customer deposits, the ECB report signalled that the financial crisis broke a broad global funding trend characterized by a strong reliance in wholesale funding sources in favour of more stable retail sources of funding. Bank funding strategies needed to be swiftly adjusted in order to expand the customer deposit base and reduce the share of wholesale funding. Greater efforts to expand the customer deposit base after the third quarter of 2008, generally implying higher funding costs, led to slowly decreasing loan-to-deposit ratios. These developments were not only due to an expansion of deposits, but also to an overall reduction in lending activity (credit crunch). Moreover, the data showed a significant increase in the share of private non-financial deposits with an original maturity of over one year as a share of total term deposits (i.e. all deposits with agreed maturity).

The analysis on the importance of debt securities as a funding instrument showed that there were significant differences across banking systems in the Euro area. Indeed, bank debt securities in the Euro area accounted for, on average, 16% of total assets at the end of 2011, albeit with a heterogeneous distribution across countries. The Euro area median and un-weighted averages were considerably lower in the

[25]Moreover, the report by ECB (2012) indicated a strong increase in the secured money market transactions.

smallest countries, reflecting a less representative proportion of debt securities in the balance sheets of banks domiciled in those economies.[26] The weighted Euro area average—which predominantly reflects developments in the largest Euro area countries—was more stable over time, although characterized by a gradual downward path since 2007. The decrease in debt issuances by European banks after the financial crisis was accompanied by a fall in securitization volumes between 2008 and 2011.

As regards the overall Eurosystem funding, it is interesting to note that, at the end of 2008, its share of total deposit liabilities for banks in some Euro area countries increased considerably, reflecting a general search for liquidity. But at the end of 2011, average recourse to central bank funding by Euro area banks in total deposit liabilities stood at roughly 5%, a level close to the one observed after Lehman's default.

Finally, the proportion of capital and reserves as a share of assets remained broadly unchanged in the pre-crisis period. It reached a low in the fourth quarter of 2008. This was to a large extent because of the strong growth in total assets. The capital-to-assets ratio, then, started growing at the beginning of 2009 on account of both the increase in capital and the decline in banks' assets.

Van Rixtel and Gasperini (2013) investigated again the impact of the financial and Euro area crises on bank funding. In particular, this paper better scrutinizes the aftermath of the Euro area financial crisis. Even if the authors signal that it is always difficult to compare banks' funding strategies, as they are often heavily influenced by bank-specific characteristics,[27] some interesting results emerge from their analysis. As documented in earlier studies, the authors find that in the search for more stable funding sources, banks sought to increase deposits; however, the worsening of the financial crisis resulted in a growing divergence in deposit growth rates across the Euro area. Most peripheral countries

---

[26]Funding through debt securities is traditionally negligible in the banking sectors of a few small Euro area countries, whereas it has represented almost a quarter of the funding structure (all liabilities) in a number of larger countries over the last decade.

[27]For example, small European banks usually resort to wholesale funding much less than do large European banks.

saw deposit withdrawals, while core countries registered strong deposits inflows: this divergence started to reduce in the third quarter of 2012. Other results reported by Van Rixtel and Gasperini (2013), relating to the conditions in the interbank market, the shift from wholesale to deposits, the difficulties in issuing bonds during the investigated period, confirm the findings from other studies. In particular, the authors indicate how the long-term wholesale funding—that represents the way to issue bonds to institutional investors—was impaired by the Euro area crisis: longer term funding markets became increasingly segmented according to bank nationality. In the process, banks from Greece, Ireland and Portugal were virtually shut out from primary bond markets, while those from Italy and Spain at times experienced severe difficulties in issuing longer term debt. Moreover, the crisis reinforced the trend towards greater recourse to secured longer term funding, especially through covered bonds.

A more recent study, that covers the entire period after the financial and Euro area crises, was published in 2016 by the ECB (see ECB 2016). In this report, the ECB indicates how the composition of Euro area banks' funding fluctuated over the past decade, reflecting changes in economic conditions, uncertainty and the monetary policy response to the crisis. Figure 1.1 can be used to summarize the result of the ECB study.[28]

Banks' overall funding grew in line with the expansion in their assets until the escalation of the financial crisis, following the collapse of Lehman Brothers and the resulting increase in uncertainty in interbank markets. Funding flows increased steadily from 2005 until the end of 2007, particularly via wholesale funding sources, which include external (non-Euro area) liabilities, interbank funding and shorter-term debt securities and tend to be more volatile than retail deposit funding. And in fact, soon after the blast of the crisis, these sources of funding suffered dramatic outflows.

[28]The ECB distinguishes between "vulnerable countries" (countries more directly affected by the crisis, namely Ireland, Greece, Spain, Italy, Cyprus, Portugal and Slovenia), and "less vulnerable countries" (the remaining Euro area countries).

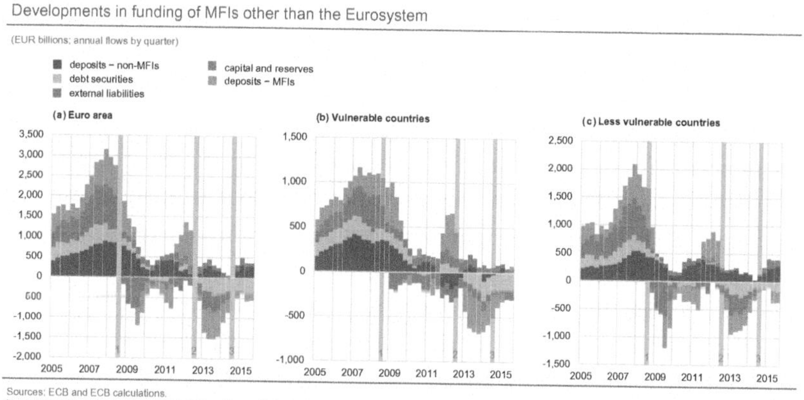

Sources: ECB and ECB calculations.
Notes: The chart highlights three periods: 1. the collapse of Lehman Brothers, 2. the announcement of OMTs, and 3. the introduction of the credit easing package. The analysis is based on aggregate MFI data: deposits from other MFIs include operations between banks belonging to the same economic group. The components constitute MFIs' main liabilities and exclude money market fund shares/units and remaining liabilities, which are composed mostly of derivatives. Data are annual flows starting in the first quarter of 2005 and ending in the third quarter of 2015. Deposits of MFIs include both interbank funding and funding from the Eurosystem.

Fig. 1.1 Developments in funding of MFIs. *Source* ECB (2016)

On the other hand, retail deposits tend to be a more stable source of funding than wholesale sources. Since the liquidity services that banks provide to depositors can incur transaction and switching costs, retail deposits are less susceptible to unanticipated withdrawals. Moreover, as withdrawals are based on individual liquidity needs they tend to be more predictable, on the basis of the law of large numbers. In addition, deposits are generally insured up to a limit and are less subject to adverse shocks related to uncertainty. Figure 1.1 reveals that, as the financial crisis intensified, deposit flows fell, but remained robust relative to the other more volatile sources of funding in both vulnerable and less vulnerable countries. Between the collapse of Lehman and the ECB's announcement of Outright Monetary Transactions (OMTs) in June 2012, deposit outflows became more pronounced in vulnerable countries, driven largely by a repatriation of funds by non-domestic depositors (both from other Euro area countries and from outside the Euro area). But after reaching a peak in mid-2012, the fragmentation in funding across the Euro area receded.

Another aspect that emerges from Fig. 1.1 is the dramatic decrease in debt securities issuance. Indeed, in vulnerable countries, as interbank funding deteriorated, banks continued to issue securities in the period 2009–2012—thanks to the fact that a proportion of these securities were covered by government guarantees. While market risks diminished in the middle of 2012, there was a second stage of negative net issuance of debt securities by banks at this time, partly reflecting the correction of excessive leverage of the financial and non-financial sectors, as well as a move towards a more comprehensive regulatory and supervisory framework. Moreover, debt securities funding was replaced by Eurosystem liquidity because the cost of the latter was more favourable.[29]

As for the Eurosystem influence on banks' funding strategies, it is interesting to mention a specific data reported by ECB. Due to the extraordinary monetary measures implemented by the ECB, and especially the introduction of the Targeted Long-Term Refinancing Operations (TLTROs), the weighted average maturity of bank borrowing from the Eurosystem increased from around 130 days before the first TLTRO was conducted to around 800 days after the settlement of the fifth TLTRO in September 2015. These numbers clearly represent the dramatic change in the role of central banks as borrowers of last resort and providers of liquidity and cast doubts on the issues that will arise soon after the interruption of the extraordinary monetary measures.

A final indication that can be extrapolated by ECB (2016) regards the level of capital as a percentage of total assets. This ratio was relatively stable in the pre-crisis period across all countries of the Euro area, but then started to significantly increase, especially in vulnerable countries. There are at least two reasons that can explain this trend: on the one hand, the level of assets decreased due to a widespread rethinking of the business model by most banks; on the other hand, capital increased in response not only to regulatory requirements but also to pressure from markets to hold larger discretionary buffers against losses. Over this period, in addition to the capital raised in private sector markets, a substantial amount of capital was also obtained through government capital injections.

---

[29]Similarly, the composition of deposits from MFIs changed as more volatile interbank liquidity was partially replaced by central bank liquidity. This trend was particularly significant in vulnerable countries.

To sum up, the ECB points out that the funding structure of Euro area banks has been altered by changes in market risk, the economic environment and monetary policy measures: there is now a greater reliance on more stable funding relative to volatile funding.

1.2.4 The Funding Structures of International Banks

With regards to funding strategies and funding structures, an interesting strand of the literature is related to the choices of international banks. As mentioned above, the size and the level of internationalization of a bank can significantly influence its funding model. Moreover, international banks can respond to financial crises in different ways compared to small–medium domestic banks, having the possibility to better and quickly reshape their funding sources. On the other hand, they can be subject to different and more complex risks. To investigate this topic, we basically refer to two studies: CGFS (2010) and Gambacorta et al. (2017).

The first aspect to be considered is that the management of risks at internationally active banks is more complex than that at local banks. Several interrelated risks are involved. Since assets and liabilities are denominated in several currencies, direct and indirect currency mismatches are generated. These are often covered by short-duration hedges that must be frequently rolled over. Differences in the duration of assets and liabilities in each currency also create distinct interest rate exposures for each currency. Moreover, banks' international operations across jurisdictions and time zones entail a broad range of legal and operational risks.

Consequently, when thinking about the funding and liquidity risks for an international bank, one needs to remember that:

a. funding risk essentially refers to a bank's (in-)ability to raise funds in the *desired currencies* on an ongoing basis;
b. liquidity risk refers to a bank's (in-)ability to raise sufficient funds in the *right currency* and *location* to finance cash outflows at any given point in time.

Other specific aspects in international banks' funding strategies regard the level of centralization/decentralization. Decentralization refers to the degree of financial autonomy of a bank's branches and subsidiaries compared to the central treasury of the banking group. In this regard, it is possible to identify the different organizational model.

In a fully decentralized model, the responsibility of funding and liquidity management is devolved to the individual local entities that, in the extreme, act as a collection of autonomous banks under common ownership. A decentralized approach sees local entities plan and raise funding for their activities and manage the associated liquidity risks. Local entities operate mainly in the host countries, and meet any shortfalls autonomously by accessing local sources; very little surplus funding is redistributed within the group, and the central treasury has only a very limited role.

At the other end of the spectrum, a fully centralized model concentrates funding and liquidity management at the central treasury on the group level. The central treasury distributes funding around the organisation, monitors compliance with strict centrally mandated mismatch limits and manages pools of liquid assets. The bank's foreign operations are not expected to fund their own balance sheets independently of the rest of the group. The centralized model is associated with extensive intragroup transfers (internal markets).[30]

In addition, as pointed out by Gambacorta et al. (2017), globally active banks can raise money abroad in two ways: directly, through cross-border liabilities from the foreign banking system (central bank and banks in the host country) or from foreign non-banks; indirectly, thanks to presence of branches and subsidiaries abroad.

In the end, the funding models of international banks can be more or less focused on raising money at home (or abroad) to fund their foreign claims. As CGFS (2010) demonstrates, there is a wide range of funding models, and the economic and financial environment of host countries

[30]Note that decentralization is different from diversification of funding.

can greatly influence the way in which international banks operate.[31] Also, microeconomic determinants are important: banks often regard the geographical funding structure as a consequence of their institution's history, which determines the overall business model that, in turn, instils a corporate culture and risk attitudes that ultimately translate into the funding approach.

The financial crisis put the funding models of international banks to the test. As we know, a strong decrease in interbank market activity characterized the aftermath of the Lehman collapse. But the intragroup positions of international banks, and the local funding of local claims, proved more resilient. Evidence from the global financial crisis is then consistent with the view that large international banks pursuing a more decentralized funding model were less affected by funding problems. Even so, centralized models demonstrated a significant flexibility due to their internal markets: for example, European banks with an established presence in the US were able to borrow from the Federal Reserve and send funds intragroup to their head offices.

The responses and adjustments to the financial crises were diverse. In general, also international banks increased their reliance on retail funding as opposed to wholesale funding, with a view to achieving more variety of sources. In addition, it became clearer that foreign liabilities could be unstable as a funding source when they are used to finance domestic credit growth.

The analysis of Gambacorta et al. (2017) points out, as well, that globally active banks increased their reliance on funding from branches and subsidiaries located abroad. In particular, banks reduced cross-border funding from unrelated banks and from non-bank entities. At the same time, they increased intragroup cross-border liabilities in an attempt to make more efficient use of their internal capital markets.

[31] For example, in less developed markets, banks often fund local credit with cross-border intragroup transfers.

1.2.5 The Determinants of Long-Term Debt Issuance

As reported in Sect. 1.2.3, the issuance of debt securities constituted an important source of funding for European banks until the beginning of the financial crisis. Later, their share on total liabilities started to decrease significantly. Yet, long-term bonds represent an interesting source of funding that can be used to improve the management of mismatching maturities in banks' balance sheets and to meet specific regulatory requirements (for instance the NSFR). In addition, if long-term bonds are placed to retail depositors, they tend to be a stable source of funding at a reasonable cost.

Nevertheless, the literature about the determinants of long-term debt issuance by banks seems to be scarce. Van Rixtel et al. (2015) tried to fill the gap with a paper specifically dedicated to this topic. Their analysis is based on a dataset of around 50,000 bonds issued by 63 banks from 14 European countries throughout the period 1999–2013; the authors test a broad set of hypotheses (bank-specific and macroeconomics), from both the corporate finance and banking literature, on the drivers of bond issuance. Their main results are the following:

- During the crisis years, there is a strong correlation between bonds issuance and total assets growth. This may be explained by the widely reported use of short-term wholesale markets in the years prior to the crisis; when access to these markets became severely limited for most banks during the crisis, they had to resort to long-term bond issuance.
- The regression coefficient of the capital ratio is significantly positive for both crisis and pre-crisis period. That confirms the risk absorption hypothesis, that is stronger capitalized banks can access bond markets at better terms and consequently will issue more bonds.
- The coefficient on the deposit ratio is negatively and significantly associated with bond issuance for both periods (pre-and post-crisis), supporting the agency costs and asymmetric information and deposit supply constraints hypotheses. The idea is that banks issue bonds to overcome deposits supply constraints: if the growth of deposit is strong, the bank does not have incentives to issue bonds.

- Moreover, bond issuance is positively and significantly associated with the loan ratio, both before and after the crisis. As loans are normally the longer maturity assets on banks' balance sheets, this result may point at a certain degree of maturity matching between long-term assets and long-term liabilities.
- Finally, the authors find the expected sign in the regression coefficient related to credit ratings: banks that are perceived to be less risky and hence have a greater credit rating issue more long-term debt than lower rated banks.[32]

Also macroeconomic and financial market conditions play an important role as determinants of bond issuance by European banks, in addition to bank-specific characteristics.[33] However, these factors do not seem to reduce the importance of bank-specific characteristics; which means that better performing banks maintained better access to longer term funding markets also during the crisis period.

1.3 The Funding Structures of European Banks: Evidence from Aggregated Data

Having illustrated the main topics regarding the banks' funding strategies, we conclude this chapter by presenting some aggregated data about the funding structures of European banks.

Our analysis is based on data retrieved from the European Central Bank Statistical Data Warehouse. This source is the official ECB's online data delivery service for statistics. Notably, it provides a variety of data (such as, interest rate and currency exchange rate time series; the balance of payments data; other macroeconomic statistics; etc.) from the Eurosystem in a harmonized manner, which ensures comparability among countries. More specifically, we are interested in aggregated

[32] But conversely, lower rated banks are more likely to issue secured debt.

[33] For example, sovereign CDS spreads were negatively correlated with bond issuance during the crisis period, suggesting the importance of country-specific risk factors.

balance sheet data of Euro area credit institutions, at the country level.[34] According to Article 4(1) of Directive 2006/48/EC,[35] a credit institution is defined as 'an undertaking whose business is to receive deposits or other repayable funds from the public and to grant credits for its own account'.

We thus started by downloading data regarding the number of credit institutions chartered in each of the 19 Euro-area countries, to have an idea of the number of banks from which our data are extracted.[36] Then, we retrieved quarterly data for about 11 years—from 2006:Q1 to 2017:Q1—regarding the following assets and liabilities categories, namely 'Loans', 'Deposits Liabilities', 'Debt Securities Issued' and 'Total Assets'.[37]

The data is available, in millions of Euro, as outstanding amounts at the end of each period. The main variable of interest for our analysis is the 'Debt Securities Issued', as it represents a proxy for the bank funding carried out via bonds issuance. Keep in mind that it is not by chance that we employ the term 'proxy'. Indeed, as we do not have disaggregated information on the bank's debt securities, we have been forced to employ a more aggregated statistics. Specifically, the category 'Debt Securities Issued'—as from the definition provided in the Regulation 1071/2013 of the European Central Bank[38]—includes the following items:

a. 'Securities that give the holder the unconditional right to a fixed or contractually determined income in the form of coupon payments

[34]The aggregated balance sheet data for Euro area credit institutions are available at the following link: http://sdw.ecb.europa.eu/browse.do?node=9691313.

[35]The Directive is available at the following link: http://eur-lex.europa.eu/legal-content/EN/TXT/?uri=CELEX%3A32006L0048.

[36]As of August 2017, the countries in the European monetary Union are the following: Austria, Belgium, Cyprus, Germany, Estonia, Spain, Finland, France, Greece, Ireland, Italy, Lithuania, Luxembourg, Latvia, Malta, Netherlands, Portugal, Slovenia, Slovakia.

[37]Note that, because the data on the 'Debt Securities Issued'—which is the main variable of interest in this chapter—was not available for Latvia, The Netherlands, and Malta, we had to exclude these three countries from our analysis.

[38]The regulation is available at the following link: https://publications.europa.eu/en/publication-detail/-/publication/accb1c9c-6cae-4b36-99ca-040e2a7566ed/language-en.

and/or a stated fixed sum at a specific date (or dates) or starting from a date defined at the time of issue;
b. Non-negotiable instruments […];
c. Subordinated debt […];
d. Hybrid instruments […]'.

Having said that, we use the information at our disposal to create the following ratios. First, we generate the Debt Securities Issued as percentage of Total Assets, to have an idea of the impact of the bank funding via bond issuance across Europe. Then, we create the Deposit Funding ratio, which is given by Deposit Liabilities over Total Assets, to control how relevant deposits are for the funding of Euro area banks. Furthermore, we construct the Loans-to-Deposit ratio, to assess the extent to which loans are financed by deposits. Finally, we also generate the Loans over Total Assets ratio to have a picture about the significance of the lending activity for the credit institutions in our sample.

Starting from Table 1.1, we observe that the number of credit institutions decreased substantially in almost every country, over time.

Notably, Italy has experienced a drop of 195 credit institutions, if we simply compare the data in 2005 with the one in 2017. This trend is obviously linked to the economic and financial conditions of the post-crisis era and testifies a general and widespread aggregation process in the banking sector.

In Table 1.2, we present some aggregated data about the outstanding amounts of debt securities issued.

The data confirm the presence of two different phases characterizing the observed period: a pre-crises stage in which we assist to an increase in the outstanding amounts of debt securities (in some countries the trend continues till the end of the Euro area debt crisis in 2012:Q3), and a second step where the volumes drop significantly. Excluding small economies, the reduction occurred from 2012:Q3 is widespread, even if remarkable differences among countries exist. Here, again, Italy is one of the countries where the decrease is quite evident (–43.3%). Other peripheral economies present the same pattern: Portugal (–84.3%), Spain (–52%). Overall, the data from our sample highlight a remarkable drop of 1,219,301 millions of Euro in the amount of outstanding debt securities from 2012:Q3 to 2017:Q1.

Table 1.1 Number of credit institutions (data at the beginning of the year). *Source* ECB Statistical Data Warehouse

Year	Austria	Belgium	Cyprus	Germany	Estonia	Spain	Finland	France	Greece	Ireland	Italy	Lithuania	Luxembourg	Latvia	Malta	Netherlands	Portugal	Slovenia	Slovakia
2005	796	104	405	2,141	9	345	362	891	62	80	785	74	161	23	16	461	195	24	21
2006	819	102	391	2,084	13	346	363	856	62	79	795	77	154	25	19	401	183	25	23
2007	809	105	336	2,041	14	352	361	827	62	78	810	78	154	27	18	346	177	27	24
2008	803	109	205	2,021	16	357	360	744	64	82	819	80	155	31	22	341	178	28	26
2009	800	107	163	1,984	17	359	357	720	66	501	813	84	153	33	23	299	172	25	26
2010	791	103	154	1,948	18	352	346	709	66	497	799	85	149	37	24	295	166	25	27
2011	780	107	144	1,930	18	336	333	677	62	488	775	87	146	39	26	290	160	25	29
2012	766	108	140	1,894	17	333	323	658	57	480	749	91	142	31	26	284	155	25	31
2013	751	104	135	1,866	34	303	313	634	52	471	709	93	141	29	28	265	150	23	28
2014	729	103	86	1,841	35	240	298	602	40	459	690	90	148	61	28	253	151	23	28
2015	705	103	57	1,807	37	223	291	496	40	446	665	89	150	59	28	217	150	24	28
2016	679	99	55	1,768	37	218	278	464	40	412	650	89	144	61	28	102	148	23	27
2017	615	92	54	1,695	37	208	274	443	38	371	590	88	142	57	27	93	145	18	28

Table 1.2 Debt securities issued (outstanding amounts at the end of the period, in millions of Euro). *Source* ECB Statistical Data Warehouse

Time/ Countries	Austria	Belgium	Cyprus	Germany	Estonia	Spain	Finland	France	Greece	Ireland	Italy	Lithuania	Luxembourg	Portugal	Slovenia	Slovakia
2006Q1		51,516	3,073	1,632,133	1,113	293,827	39,389	726,488	581	131,481	504,176	494	72,922	18,664	1,447	
2006Q2		51,086	3,998	1,641,113	1,138	314,893	40,450	742,948	690	142,888	516,036	523	73,621	18,474	1,405	
2006Q3		51,745	4,319	1,639,591	1,148	338,562	42,529	781,038	744	156,808	522,230	585	72,538	18,710	1,448	
2006Q4		50,895	3,859	1,636,731	1,155	351,946	43,988	803,973	809	170,621	542,323	465	78,269	20,088	1,468	
2007Q1		54,953	3,767	1,659,713	1,078	378,057	46,815	841,647	797	182,719	563,944	538	78,507	22,712	1,480	
2007Q2		57,903	4,740	1,670,395	1,088	406,134	46,621	878,253	785	185,643	577,789	690	78,320	31,256	1,509	
2007Q3		61,026	4,751	1,651,546	1,074	428,309	48,741	930,318	858	173,168	580,080	728	79 276	32,453	1,516	
2007Q4		64,756	4,911	1,637,606	1,128	424,076	49,625	984,063	1,086	166,069	613,129	782	77,937	35,622	1,528	
2008Q1		68,750	4,694	1,622,325	1,089	412,698	50,216	1,007,315	1,975	161,636	652,519	885	69,775	38,838	1,528	
2008Q2		72,898	4,459	1,641,376	1,021	435,462	51,153	1,027,221	2,551	155,570	698,262	964	72,305	48,102	1,539	
2008Q3		74,021	5,224	1,642,195	1,013	423,294	53,799	1,051,798	3,440	152,133	714,289	847	78,255	51,206	1,538	
2008Q4	253,752	68,971	4,800	1,609,937	965	397,282	56,184	1,086,673	2,960	146,704	737,214	747	73,016	54,022	1,761	3,559
2009Q1	252,447	70,366	4,804	1,580,157	888	413,366	54,152	1,103,347	2,704	147,819	784,527	659	75,612	61,370	2,022	3,376
2009Q2	253,435	76,368	4,785	1,570,984	876	437,557	52,475	1,085,797	3,663	143,574	805,983	577	70,667	69,687	1,854	3,400
2009Q3	256,545	88,835	5,274	1,543,331	850	441,843	52,092	1,042,654	3,283	148,142	813,402	582	69,640	72,250	3,863	3,583
2009Q4	252,043	87,755	4,674	1,500,543	88	438,242	51,246	1,040,943	2,404	143,257	818,278	616	72,385	79,415	3,829	3,529
2010Q1	253,092	85,075	4,684	1,503,197	54	446,255	52,977	1,090,396	2,894	154,106	813,263	694	70,350	82,749	3,821	3,426
2010Q2	251,910	80,484	4,498	1,487,228	28	421,488	57,169	1,101,447	15,011	150,894	805,012	515	72,404	82,138	5,033	3,433
2010Q3	249,871	78,443	2,513	1,440,289	25	422,566	57,078	1,097,334	3,476	127,776	813,151	458	68,253	84,497	5,020	3,407
2010Q4	244,276	70,784	2,562	1,407,804	35	431,802	59,854	1,102,352	3,425	108,647	804,722	365	63,698	82,913	5,056	3,456
2011Q1	245,067	76,859	2,563	1,373,357	26	444,954	58,559	1,125,677	3,452	100,376	827,605	366	59,079	84,144	5,332	3,577
2011Q2	243,511	75,266	2,658	1,360,090	19	436,111	63,661	1,136,388	2,735	98,472	837,017	423	60,217	85,556	4,732	3,528
2011Q3	242,641	71,615	2,674	1,352,449	16	424,149	68,795	1,186,255	3,000	95,738	853,379	528	59,525	89,864	4,564	3,572
2011Q4	239,000	70,395	2,677	1,345,698	16	434,127	70,277	1,198,475	1,568	90,848	907,175	334	58,471	97,171	4,232	3,529
2012Q1	233,093	72,802	2,176	1,305,666	10	441,586	73,801	1,242,445	1,953	79,546	952,863	325	57,750	94,499	3,876	3,611
2012Q2	226,779	71,006	2,095	1,291,653	7	410,399	79,813	1,222,424	3,688	74,726	946,306	332	57,329	97,213	3,644	3,700
2012Q3	227,439	61,761	1,771	1,277,184	7	400,984	81,297	1,224,407	3,039	73,910	954,749	323	54,812	99,324	2,604	3,890
2012Q4	213,155	60,516	1,746	1,233,087	2	394,143	79,525	1,176,210	3,173	76,142	952,265	326	52,635	98,886	2,439	3,504
2013Q1	205,463	60,140	1,822	1,201,471	2	376,297	80,285	1,163,534	1,572	73,103	924,301	326	51,978	95,697	2,563	3,670
2013Q2	204,083	60,164	491	1,165,963	1	335,670	81,824	1,146,320	1,372	66,940	911,122	205	49,556	89,803	2,142	3,588
2013Q3	197,960	60,211	500	1,139,717	1	313,896	84,413	1,120,597	1,471	59,548	889,672	173	48,055	87,291	1,978	3,651
2013Q4	198,520	59,646	503	1,115,206	1	297,229	82,421	1,073,024	1,464	58,107	875,806	123	47,531	85,665	1,624	3,712

(continued)

Table 1.2 (continued)

Time/ Countries	Austria	Belgium	Cyprus	Germany	Estonia	Spain	Finland	France	Greece	Ireland	Italy	Lithuania	Luxembourg	Portugal	Slovenia	Slovakia
2014Q1	194,032	61,716	485	1,090,419	1	282,209	88,781	1,101,954	1,444	58,835	828,818	126	48,918	80,381	1,602	3,812
2014Q2	191,144	61,634	410	1,085,487	2	269,989	88,817	1,096,733	2,638	57,941	800,931	115	48,484	72,310	1,523	3,836
2014Q3	188,968	61,020	386	1,084,727	3	257,942	88,603	1,109,231	2,647	61,475	765,144	102	47,270	66,555	1,725	3,880
2014Q4	172,769	60,481	367	1,077,562	4	259,705	89,309	1,067,920	1,900	57,208	727,031	57	45,958	60,675	1,638	3,946
2015Q1	170,002	64,216	654	1,108,019	4	244,013	92,228	1,087,802	1,898	50,335	687,362	44	50,399	60,551	1,563	3,939
2015Q2	165,229	62,437	633	1,076,079	7	233,747	91,885	1,054,646	1,823	50,569	656,515	43	46,097	59,171	895	4,119
2015Q3	161,375	61,250	631	1,060,486	8	230,987	93,538	1,023,374	1,816	51,307	630,251	41	44,246	56,025	1,203	4,151
2015Q4	160,050	63,350	630	1,017,672	9	231,835	93,860	1,013,122	5,344	50,039	621,790	44	44,737	55,029	1,123	4,272
2016Q1	153,892	64,786	640	1,014,670	9	217,066	94,080	1,011,340	5,314	49,416	585,634	38	42,526	54,187	824	4,452
2016Q2	152,420	64,179	347	1,023,885	9	218,746	94,663	1,017,148	5,311	49,722	582,542	30	46,475	53,810	815	4,599
2016Q3	147,174	66,393	302	1,011,078	13	211,811	93,388	1,026,816	5,310	47,869	569,593	18	47,759	50,208	787	4,515
2016Q4	138,627	78,300	276	1,030,346	13	206,891	92,094	1,031,383	2,442	40,042	558,006	11	48,524	46,696	789	4,607
2017Q1	138,421	79,727	517	1,045,706	19	192,174	88,617	1,035,732	2,257	52,975	540,890	5	49,967	15,573	768	4,852

Table 1.3 provides information about the debt securities issued as percentage of total assets. Indeed, it is important to understand whether the observed decrease in bonds volumes can be explained by a parallel reduction in the overall size of banks after the two crises, or whether this simply happened because bonds have been substituted by other forms of funding.

We note that the importance of bonds as a funding source has clearly diminished in many countries: in Italy, for instance, the percentage of bonds over total assets was 22.52% in 2012:Q3, and 13.61% in 2017:Q1 (–39.46%). Again, Portugal and Spain show similar trends to Italy, while in France and Germany the decreased weight of bonds as a bank funding source appears less pronounced.

Figure 1.2 restricts the analysis to Italy, France, Germany and Spain. Interestingly, the level of debt securities issued over total assets is almost coincident for Italy, France and Germany, even if the paths followed throughout the observed period are quite different. In Germany, the share of debt securities to total assets constantly diminished since 2006. In Italy, we observe a peak in 2012:Q3 and then a drastic decrease. In France, instead, the share of bonds remained more stable.

In contrast, if we consider deposits, as represented in Table 1.4 (amounts in euro) and in Table 1.5 (percentages of total assets), we observe a totally different situation.

Data displayed in Table 1.4 highlight that, since the beginning of the observed period, the level of banks' deposits increased in almost every country, notably in Italy and France. Overall, the share of deposits over total assets increased in the majority of countries, testifying a growing reliance of banks on deposits (that has been also documented by other studies previously mentioned). When we restrict the analysis to the four largest economies and plot the related deposits to total assets ratios in Fig. 1.3, we observe that the increasing importance of deposits as a funding choice was significantly high in Italy; whereas in Germany, after the drop registered in the period 2010–2012, the share of deposits over total assets returned almost back to the pre-crisis levels.

Another interesting aspect can be extrapolated by the analysis of the Loan-to-Deposit ratio presented in Table 1.6. As we mentioned above, Le Leslé (2012) found that this ratio was unfavourable for European

Table 1.3 Debt securities issued (as % of total assets). *Source* Authors' elaboration on data from the ECB Statistical Data Warehouse

Time/ Countries	Austria	Belgium	Cyprus	Germany	Estonia	Spain	Finland	France	Greece	Ireland	Italy	Lithuania	Luxembourg	Portugal	Slovenia	Slovakia
2006Q1		0.0486	0.0478	0.2341	0.0866	0.1325	0.1635	0.1369	0.0020	0.1330	0.1978	0.0355	0.0886	0.0502	0.0458	
2006Q2		0.0480	0.0594	0.2331	0.0828	0.1366	0.1650	0.1384	0.0023	0.1360	0.1989	0.0346	0.0897	0.0487	0.0428	
2006Q3		0.0488	0.0599	0.2327	0.0829	0.1409	0.1727	0.1394	0.0024	0.1436	0.1955	0.0378	0.0860	0.0491	0.0432	
2006Q4		0.0454	0.0504	0.2298	0.0751	0.1393	0.1725	0.1404	0.0026	0.1448	0.1942	0.0268	0.0932	0.0506	0.0421	
2007Q1		0.0480	0.0470	0.2288	0.0661	0.1446	0.1758	0.1371	0.0024	0.1510	0.1950	0.0291	0.0912	0.0575	0.0410	
2007Q2		0.0476	0.0547	0.2274	0.0590	0.1471	0.1756	0.1376	0.0023	0.1444	0.1915	0.0351	0.0889	0.0752	0.0392	
2007Q3		0.0504	0.0519	0.2211	0.0557	0.1500	0.1770	0.1434	0.0024	0.1364	0.1912	0.0340	0.0874	0.0765	0.0370	
2007Q4		0.0499	0.0529	0.2165	0.0547	0.1411	0.1725	0.1473	0.0028	0.1242	0.1840	0.0328	0.0851	0.0811	0.0351	
2008Q1		0.0527	0.0502	0.2131	0.0517	0.1357	0.1617	0.1465	0.0050	0.1154	0.1926	0.0366	0.0743	0.0883	0.0338	
2008Q2		0.0535	0.0468	0.2142	0.0473	0.1367	0.1554	0.1501	0.0061	0.1088	0.1985	0.0380	0.0767	0.1052	0.0324	
2008Q3		0.0526	0.0487	0.2086	0.0466	0.1302	0.1578	0.1510	0.0079	0.1052	0.2004	0.0319	0.0788	0.1097	0.0319	
2008Q4	0.2402	0.0543	0.0406	0.2044	0.0437	0.1175	0.1463	0.1504	0.0064	0.1039	0.2028	0.0281	0.0784	0.1120	0.0359	0.0557
2009Q1	0.2399	0.0566	0.0358	0.2036	0.0413	0.1210	0.1405	0.1555	0.0057	0.1059	0.2115	0.0252	0.0858	0.1242	0.0406	0.0628
2009Q2	0.2425	0.0641	0.0338	0.2041	0.0410	0.1261	0.1399	0.1493	0.0075	0.1030	0.2182	0.0224	0.0829	0.1375	0.0367	0.0627
2009Q3	0.2468	0.0765	0.0374	0.2056	0.0403	0.1296	0.1398	0.1449	0.0068	0.1105	0.2216	0.0224	0.0852	0.1426	0.0733	0.0653
2009Q4	0.2453	0.0759	0.0335	0.2021	0.0041	0.1276	0.1322	0.1455	0.0049	0.1082	0.2217	0.0235	0.0908	0.1527	0.0717	0.0648
2010Q1	0.2490	0.0743	0.0323	0.2020	0.0026	0.1301	0.1327	0.1458	0.0058	0.1170	0.2189	0.0270	0.0901	0.1561	0.0725	0.0626
2010Q2	0.2455	0.0663	0.0264	0.1949	0.0013	0.1212	0.1221	0.1423	0.0276	0.1124	0.2041	0.0199	0.0888	0.1496	0.0918	0.0608
2010Q3	0.2545	0.0671	0.0182	0.1953	0.0012	0.1215	0.1247	0.1424	0.0066	0.0974	0.2054	0.0179	0.0876	0.1524	0.0936	0.0614
2010Q4	0.2502	0.0625	0.0190	0.1697	0.0017	0.1247	0.1273	0.1487	0.0067	0.0930	0.2141	0.0142	0.0828	0.1484	0.0954	0.0613
2011Q1	0.2485	0.0705	0.0194	0.1729	0.0013	0.1290	0.1210	0.1548	0.0069	0.0925	0.2204	0.0146	0.0771	0.1512	0.0978	0.0630
2011Q2	0.2460	0.0687	0.0203	0.1727	0.0010	0.1230	0.1300	0.1533	0.0055	0.0962	0.2215	0.0166	0.0782	0.1504	0.0897	0.0614
2011Q3	0.2411	0.0596	0.0195	0.1595	0.0008	0.1191	0.1150	0.1471	0.0061	0.0915	0.2160	0.0203	0.0739	0.1570	0.0866	0.0610
2011Q4	0.2369	0.0588	0.0203	0.1605	0.0008	0.1202	0.1110	0.1493	0.0033	0.0886	0.2248	0.0135	0.0734	0.1695	0.0808	0.0612
2012Q1	0.2308	0.0628	0.0167	0.1533	0.0005	0.1186	0.1156	0.1541	0.0045	0.0838	0.2302	0.0134	0.0733	0.1629	0.0722	0.0607
2012Q2	0.2250	0.0598	0.0157	0.1497	0.0004	0.1104	0.1224	0.1483	0.0084	0.0784	0.2256	0.0138	0.0726	0.1690	0.0686	0.0628
2012Q3	0.2285	0.0522	0.0132	0.1492	0.0004	0.1105	0.1244	0.1496	0.0070	0.0810	0.2252	0.0134	0.0717	0.1762	0.0505	0.0653
2012Q4	0.2187	0.0558	0.0136	0.1500	0.0001	0.1103	0.1332	0.1526	0.0072	0.0873	0.2261	0.0134	0.0714	0.1779	0.0480	0.0588
2013Q1	0.2169	0.0550	0.0156	0.1491	0.0001	0.1071	0.1443	0.1425	0.0037	0.0909	0.2194	0.0133	0.0687	0.1752	0.0505	0.0613
2013Q2	0.2167	0.0567	0.0049	0.1490	0.0001	0.0989	0.1560	0.1422	0.0033	0.0852	0.2190	0.0087	0.0657	0.1691	0.0429	0.0600
2013Q3	0.2149	0.0563	0.0055	0.1485	0.0001	0.0958	0.1625	0.1420	0.0035	0.0779	0.2161	0.0073	0.0649	0.1694	0.0401	0.0612
2013Q4	0.2173	0.0584	0.0056	0.1482	0.0001	0.0946	0.1579	0.1420	0.0036	0.0785	0.2169	0.0051	0.0664	0.1671	0.0351	0.0609
2014Q1	0.2131	0.0594	0.0053	0.1452	0.0000	0.0905	0.1654	0.1445	0.0036	0.0814	0.2044	0.0052	0.0680	0.1621	0.0347	0.0618

(continued)

Table 1.3 (continued)

Time/ Countries	Austria	Belgium	Cyprus	Germany	Estonia	Spain	Finland	France	Greece	Ireland	Italy	Lithuania	Luxembourg	Portugal	Slovenia	Slovakia
2014Q2	0.2104	0.0575	0.0045	0.1431	0.0001	0.0872	0.1618	0.1427	0.0067	0.0799	0.1992	0.0048	0.0659	0.1485	0.0337	0.0618
2014Q3	0.2070	0.0557	0.0043	0.1401	0.0001	0.0841	0.1551	0.1418	0.0067	0.0870	0.1909	0.0042	0.0623	0.1386	0.0385	0.0611
2014Q4	0.1972	0.0549	0.0040	0.1382	0.0002	0.0876	0.1551	0.1355	0.0048	0.0835	0.1811	0.0022	0.0622	0.1299	0.0376	0.0615
2015Q1	0.1923	0.0543	0.0069	0.1356	0.0002	0.0819	0.1453	0.1322	0.0048	0.0739	0.1687	0.0018	0.0632	0.1308	0.0363	0.0606
2015Q2	0.1904	0.0561	0.0070	0.1380	0.0003	0.0808	0.1534	0.1339	0.0047	0.0774	0.1650	0.0018	0.0611	0.1284	0.0214	0.0626
2015Q3	0.1881	0.0553	0.0070	0.1355	0.0004	0.0808	0.1567	0.1303	0.0048	0.0822	0.1600	0.0017	0.0582	0.1243	0.0288	0.0616
2015Q4	0.1874	0.0597	0.0069	0.1328	0.0004	0.0822	0.1699	0.1294	0.0139	0.0816	0.1589	0.0018	0.0599	0.1231	0.0270	0.0619
2016Q1	0.1796	0.0581	0.0074	0.1304	0.0004	0.0773	0.1569	0.1271	0.0139	0.0818	0.1481	0.0015	0.0554	0.1226	0.0203	0.0634
2016Q2	0.1793	0.0564	0.0041	0.1293	0.0004	0.0772	0.1585	0.1243	0.0144	0.0830	0.1464	0.0012	0.0600	0.1222	0.0204	0.0650
2016Q3	0.1752	0.0591	0.0036	0.1286	0.0005	0.0765	0.1579	0.1269	0.0145	0.0803	0.1449	0.0007	0.0641	0.1154	0.0199	0.0627
2016Q4	0.1641	0.0712	0.0032	0.1323	0.0005	0.0761	0.1694	0.1292	0.0070	0.0678	0.1424	0.0004	0.0635	0.1097	0.0197	0.0630
2017Q1	0.1617	0.0715	0.0059	0.1320	0.0008	0.0713	0.1907	0.1257	0.0066	0.0911	0.1361	0.0002	0.0639	0.0386	0.0189	0.0651

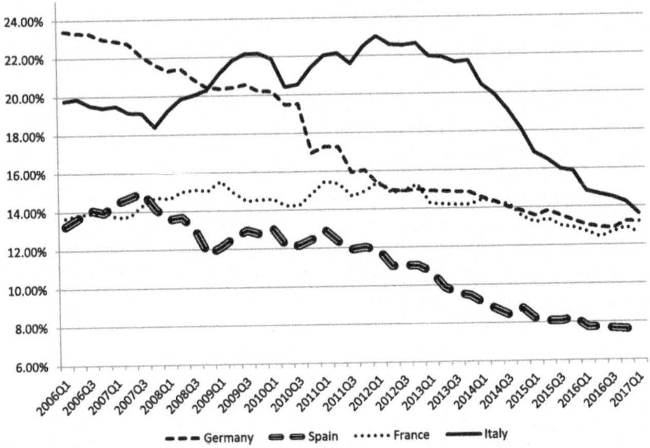

Fig. 1.2 Debt securities as % of total assets, selected countries. *Source* Authors' elaboration on data from the ECB Statistical Data Warehouse

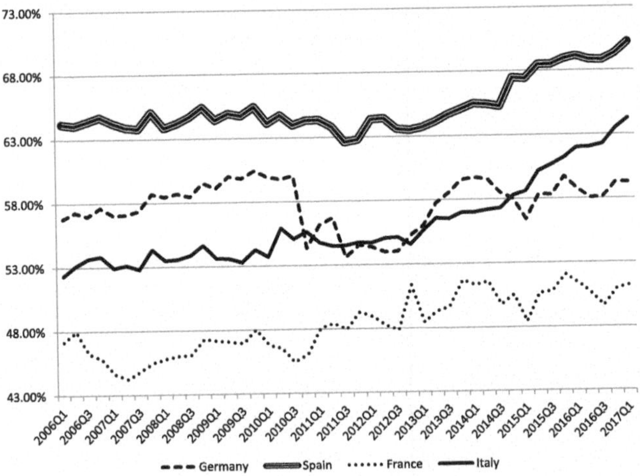

Fig. 1.3 Deposits as percentage of total assets, selected countries. *Source* Authors' elaboration on data from the ECB Statistical Data Warehouse

banks compared to their peers located in American and Emerging economies, even though it was gradually diminishing. Overall, our data show that the downward trend continued until 2017, and this was

Table 1.4 Deposit liabilities (outstanding amounts at the end of the period, in millions of Euro). *Source* ECB Statistical Data Warehouse

Time/ Country	Austria	Belgium	Cyprus	Germany	Estonia	Spain	Finland	France	Greece	Ireland	Italy	Lithuania	Luxem-bourg	Portugal	Slovenia	Slovakia
2006Q1		593,480	34,371	3,958,747	6,490	1,423,784	100,250	2,504,070	185,561	444,752	1,333,695	8,808	455,931	224,625	24,323	
2006Q2		601,750	36,277	4,034,011	6,967	1,477,277	103,111	2,576,053	191,785	468,616	1,378,051	9,490	459,291	229,206	25,752	
2006Q3		593,895	38,068	4,013,572	7,355	1,547,112	106,705	2,591,135	194,471	477,674	1,433,863	9,972	472,035	222,155	26,147	
2006Q4		639,414	38,524	4,103,889	8,153	1,635,286	108,097	2,625,193	202,579	496,661	1,503,906	11,126	467,463	231,005	27,222	
2007Q1		636,751	41,194	4,138,055	8,372	1,680,280	109,273	2,740,731	212,484	489,448	1,531,448	11,620	491,226	228,642	27,672	
2007Q2		644,814	43,694	4,192,895	8,561	1,764,782	107,309	2,824,969	220,783	512,424	1,603,701	11,769	505,106	236,579	28,974	
2007Q3		638,093	47,240	4,286,274	8,776	1,821,955	109,772	2,912,034	226,482	489,184	1,602,398	12,243	521,182	243,334	30,954	
2007Q4		695,933	48,378	4,438,712	9,342	1,956,154	115,731	3,040,542	248,056	535,882	1,811,426	13,580	523,741	255,651	33,333	
2008Q1		704,395	48,009	4,450,642	9,768	1,941,923	123,853	3,149,766	255,535	529,103	1,812,178	13,561	560,662	257,187	34,906	
2008Q2		710,579	49,840	4,498,831	10,225	2,045,928	128,079	3,149,939	275,796	563,380	1,884,629	14,230	560,780	263,555	36,889	
2008Q3		788,060	61,358	4,601,546	10,289	2,103,161	134,923	3,209,862	287,789	613,372	1,920,454	14,913	580,704	273,647	37,607	
2008Q4	590,611	686,805	74,852	4,686,919	10,360	2,212,767	135,251	3,419,165	324,048	693,969	1,986,665	14,135	556,052	288,753	38,430	48,876
2009Q1	585,476	671,828	89,569	4,587,131	10,391	2,200,338	131,198	3,347,704	341,314	740,618	1,989,169	13,927	511,624	287,130	38,847	40,377
2009Q2	570,427	670,825	96,134	4,621,066	10,525	2,253,932	133,705	3,425,185	358,828	737,611	1,979,737	13,950	510,589	292,402	39,779	40,928
2009Q3	556,333	643,666	94,585	4,493,852	10,461	2,208,049	131,910	3,378,643	343,730	674,136	1,956,596	13,970	482,194	289,166	39,734	41,204
2009Q4	556,731	634,438	92,788	4,488,164	10,980	2,246,960	136,330	3,436,586	357,365	663,593	2,002,925	14,722	479,691	292,101	40,525	41,316
2010Q1	541,174	622,135	96,069	4,462,173	10,918	2,200,266	136,825	3,499,324	368,591	652,072	1,995,753	14,879	456,788	291,176	39,609	40,584
2010Q2	551,084	651,571	120,949	4,561,727	11,132	2,252,552	140,671	3,602,549	373,278	686,272	2,206,553	15,060	464,522	315,891	39,994	42,175
2010Q3	523,822	612,822	90,861	4,428,739	11,104	2,225,005	138,635	3,501,595	373,034	720,092	2,180,878	14,974	450,523	321,696	38,716	41,218
2010Q4	525,107	625,008	87,540	4,508,361	11,443	2,227,828	143,876	3,414,117	362,518	680,538	2,091,319	15,014	452,133	332,147	38,115	42,407
2011Q1	533,048	600,608	82,243	4,461,812	11,371	2,220,479	149,660	3,496,537	344,031	642,578	2,056,776	15,079	457,241	332,060	38,917	41,375
2011Q2	542,638	622,513	78,829	4,464,986	11,686	2,263,605	150,966	3,590,900	359,147	586,250	2,059,446	15,333	459,335	342,509	37,776	42,086
2011Q3	548,088	663,671	84,464	4,545,069	11,876	2,230,006	155,314	3,869,076	346,886	576,520	2,154,052	15,657	476,433	341,887	37,653	42,472
2011Q4	545,460	671,923	79,169	4,575,268	11,801	2,269,008	159,868	3,960,045	342,349	570,515	2,208,762	15,121	465,117	340,646	37,938	42,161
2012Q1	558,569	659,092	75,052	4,632,676	11,900	2,396,829	163,957	3,948,662	328,970	524,891	2,265,238	14,961	455,204	349,371	38,846	43,691
2012Q2	565,003	664,514	81,209	4,659,513	12,391	2,396,637	170,352	3,977,767	322,355	528,081	2,310,068	15,151	454,598	338,845	38,535	43,493
2012Q3	551,344	668,102	80,427	4,626,275	12,678	2,307,722	176,351	3,917,803	318,412	496,558	2,337,319	15,519	445,911	327,432	37,292	43,641
2012Q4	532,720	636,940	73,587	4,542,837	12,779	2,269,793	175,282	3,959,268	317,146	465,736	2,297,600	15,745	431,244	321,182	36,837	44,199
2013Q1	520,608	636,855	64,269	4,513,149	12,677	2,238,400	177,742	3,959,908	288,056	418,423	2,343,506	15,671	445,376	314,278	36,911	43,799
2013Q2	518,756	645,081	56,385	4,519,467	12,826	2,175,872	178,375	3,976,262	273,905	409,278	2,354,164	15,236	451,860	309,033	36,356	44,119
2013Q3	510,399	626,421	53,854	4,492,790	12,880	2,120,570	179,256	3,921,611	275,345	397,908	2,326,324	15,357	443,977	308,364	35,881	43,762
2013Q4	511,215	617,927	52,489	4,482,598	13,396	2,045,789	183,439	3,907,144	266,776	385,690	2,301,346	15,812	430,031	308,545	32,207	44,873
2014Q1	504,018	625,224	52,068	4,483,995	13,678	2,043,449	188,812	3,916,848	255,625	380,556	2,311,742	16,029	428,282	295,621	32,026	44,559

(continued)

Table 1.4 (continued)

Time/ Country	Austria	Belgium	Cyprus	Germany	Estonia	Spain	Finland	France	Greece	Ireland	Italy	Lithuania	Luxem-bourg	Portugal	Slovenia	Slovakia
2014Q2	505,096	637,240	51,859	4,522,251	14,110	2,026,932	190,377	3,965,271	239,225	367,829	2,299,256	16,188	443,375	291,737	31,352	45,169
2014Q3	511,934	639,996	49,562	4,529,848	14,211	2,003,060	190,783	3,894,694	238,663	353,726	2,296,856	16,642	460,067	288,208	30,658	46,147
2014Q4	503,957	619,944	48,866	4,525,100	14,752	2,001,518	186,249	3,984,240	243,789	349,332	2,339,311	18,375	450,100	285,676	30,095	46,470
2015Q1	507,977	644,440	48,429	4,607,902	14,678	2,007,892	199,623	3,985,891	263,013	347,252	2,388,528	17,509	482,317	279,615	29,528	46,732
2015Q2	504,008	630,772	46,339	4,548,058	15,254	1,982,093	204,173	3,989,770	263,851	336,221	2,394,183	17,567	462,047	282,101	29,382	47,646
2015Q3	502,133	626,324	46,191	4,562,809	15,274	1,958,912	200,681	3,989,890	257,960	333,341	2,390,018	17,704	465,944	280,510	29,045	49,286
2015Q4	504,841	619,631	45,701	4,577,398	14,252	1,943,921	194,901	4,080,104	249,711	328,624	2,396,150	18,433	462,124	281,691	29,240	50,992
2016Q1	507,352	633,702	45,700	4,575,142	14,555	1,942,742	205,172	4,093,389	241,668	324,588	2,451,008	17,864	476,688	278,821	28,998	50,964
2016Q2	504,770	647,385	46,176	4,595,112	14,918	1,950,456	202,397	4,147,310	230,933	315,573	2,468,048	18,516	473,948	280,490	28,425	51,523
2016Q3	500,743	647,857	46,504	4,569,832	15,035	1,904,442	201,376	4,015,478	222,754	315,467	2,447,326	18,951	442,178	278,935	28,500	53,077
2016Q4	507,098	633,205	46,970	4,618,702	15,624	1,884,977	202,892	4,066,976	212,378	322,228	2,487,861	20,276	448,828	278,357	29,374	54,172
2017Q1	522,159	656,566	46,842	4,696,274	15,715	1,894,213	203,414	4,220,447	202,053	313,243	2,554,881	20,067	471,478	281,741	29,983	55,113

Table 1.5 Deposit funding ratio (i.e. Deposits over Total Assets). *Source* Authors' elaboration on data from the ECB Statistical Data Warehouse

Time/ Country	Austria	Belgium	Cyprus	Germany	Estonia	Spain	Finland	France	Greece	Ireland	Italy	Lithuania	Luxembourg	Portugal	Slovenia	Slovakia
2006Q1		0.5595	0.5344	0.5678	0.5049	0.6420	0.4162	0.4717	0.6463	0.4499	0.5233	0.6333	0.5540	0.6044	0.7704	
2006Q2		0.5657	0.5393	0.5729	0.5071	0.6407	0.4205	0.4800	0.6497	0.4459	0.5311	0.6274	0.5597	0.6047	0.7839	
2006Q3		0.5599	0.5282	0.5697	0.5314	0.6437	0.4333	0.4624	0.6352	0.4373	0.5366	0.6445	0.5593	0.5834	0.7799	
2006Q4		0.5699	0.5028	0.5763	0.5301	0.6472	0.4238	0.4583	0.6421	0.4216	0.5384	0.6414	0.5568	0.5817	0.7815	
2007Q1		0.5566	0.5136	0.5704	0.5131	0.6425	0.4103	0.4464	0.6405	0.4046	0.5294	0.6291	0.5707	0.5788	0.7666	
2007Q2		0.5301	0.5041	0.5709	0.4646	0.6391	0.4042	0.4425	0.6386	0.3987	0.5314	0.5988	0.5733	0.5695	0.7524	
2007Q3		0.5274	0.5165	0.5739	0.4549	0.6380	0.3987	0.4488	0.6391	0.3853	0.5282	0.5710	0.5747	0.5734	0.7564	
2007Q4		0.5362	0.5208	0.5869	0.4534	0.6509	0.4022	0.4550	0.6469	0.4007	0.5437	0.5702	0.5721	0.5817	0.7666	
2008Q1		0.5396	0.5138	0.5846	0.4636	0.6385	0.3988	0.4581	0.6457	0.3776	0.5349	0.5601	0.5971	0.5845	0.7721	
2008Q2		0.5218	0.5229	0.5870	0.4736	0.6420	0.3892	0.4602	0.6610	0.3942	0.5358	0.5604	0.5949	0.5763	0.7771	
2008Q3		0.5596	0.5721	0.5845	0.4738	0.6470	0.3957	0.4609	0.6612	0.4241	0.5388	0.5621	0.5846	0.5865	0.7802	
2008Q4	0.5591	0.5405	0.6336	0.5951	0.4687	0.6544	0.3523	0.4732	0.7011	0.4914	0.5466	0.5326	0.5969	0.5989	0.7844	0.7651
2009Q1	0.5564	0.5399	0.6678	0.5910	0.4828	0.6442	0.3404	0.4717	0.7241	0.5304	0.5363	0.5326	0.5807	0.5812	0.7791	0.7515
2009Q2	0.5459	0.5632	0.6800	0.6004	0.4931	0.6494	0.3564	0.4710	0.7332	0.5290	0.5360	0.5413	0.5990	0.5770	0.7869	0.7553
2009Q3	0.5351	0.5546	0.6711	0.5987	0.4962	0.6475	0.3539	0.4696	0.7161	0.5031	0.5330	0.5371	0.5897	0.5705	0.7538	0.7512
2009Q4	0.5419	0.5491	0.6658	0.6046	0.5146	0.6545	0.3517	0.4803	0.7281	0.5014	0.5427	0.5624	0.6015	0.5616	0.7590	0.7586
2010Q1	0.5324	0.5435	0.6630	0.5996	0.5195	0.6415	0.3427	0.4679	0.7341	0.4952	0.5371	0.5795	0.5849	0.5493	0.7514	0.7416
2010Q2	0.5371	0.5365	0.7088	0.5979	0.5313	0.6477	0.3003	0.4654	0.6866	0.5110	0.5595	0.5810	0.5694	0.5754	0.7298	0.7473
2010Q3	0.5335	0.5240	0.6583	0.6004	0.5386	0.6398	0.3029	0.4544	0.7070	0.5490	0.5508	0.5857	0.5779	0.5803	0.7219	0.7427
2010Q4	0.5379	0.5517	0.6486	0.5435	0.5626	0.6433	0.3060	0.4605	0.7056	0.5826	0.5564	0.5849	0.5878	0.5944	0.7191	0.7522
2011Q1	0.5405	0.5507	0.6218	0.5616	0.5800	0.6437	0.3091	0.4809	0.6925	0.5923	0.5477	0.6004	0.5968	0.5967	0.7139	0.7292
2011Q2	0.5481	0.5678	0.6010	0.5669	0.5888	0.6382	0.3083	0.4845	0.7160	0.5730	0.5449	0.6010	0.5962	0.6021	0.7159	0.7329
2011Q3	0.5447	0.5520	0.6159	0.5359	0.6155	0.6262	0.2595	0.4797	0.7088	0.5511	0.5451	0.6018	0.5911	0.5974	0.7146	0.7248
2011Q4	0.5407	0.5616	0.6014	0.5455	0.6205	0.6280	0.2526	0.4932	0.7190	0.5561	0.5474	0.6123	0.5838	0.5942	0.7240	0.7315
2012Q1	0.5531	0.5681	0.5756	0.5439	0.6241	0.6437	0.2569	0.4896	0.7571	0.5532	0.5473	0.6183	0.5775	0.6023	0.7235	0.7344
2012Q2	0.5607	0.5594	0.6078	0.5399	0.6456	0.6444	0.2613	0.4827	0.7379	0.5540	0.5506	0.6316	0.5757	0.5891	0.7256	0.7384
2012Q3	0.5540	0.5651	0.5978	0.5403	0.6498	0.6360	0.2699	0.4787	0.7298	0.5444	0.5513	0.6438	0.5836	0.5808	0.7239	0.7331
2012Q4	0.5467	0.5874	0.5743	0.5527	0.6497	0.6351	0.2936	0.5138	0.7185	0.5337	0.5456	0.6452	0.5846	0.5779	0.7257	0.7420
2013Q1	0.5496	0.5820	0.5491	0.5602	0.6622	0.6372	0.3194	0.4849	0.6760	0.5203	0.5563	0.6393	0.5886	0.5752	0.7273	0.7321
2013Q2	0.5509	0.6077	0.5587	0.5774	0.6690	0.6413	0.3400	0.4931	0.6549	0.5208	0.5658	0.6453	0.5988	0.5820	0.7276	0.7374
2013Q3	0.5540	0.5852	0.5888	0.5853	0.6722	0.6469	0.3451	0.4969	0.6556	0.5208	0.5651	0.6492	0.5995	0.5985	0.7274	0.7330
2013Q4	0.5597	0.6055	0.5813	0.5957	0.6714	0.6508	0.3515	0.5170	0.6560	0.5208	0.5699	0.6578	0.6006	0.6018	0.6959	0.7362
2014Q1	0.5536	0.6019	0.5709	0.5972	0.6758	0.6550	0.3518	0.5135	0.6328	0.5267	0.5700	0.6660	0.5955	0.5962	0.6945	0.7219

(continued)

Table 1.5 (continued)

Time/ Country	Austria	Belgium	Cyprus	Germany	Estonia	Spain	Finland	France	Greece	Ireland	Italy	Lithuania	Luxembourg	Portugal	Slovenia	Slovakia
2014Q2	0.5561	0.5941	0.5654	0.5962	0.6784	0.6544	0.3468	0.5161	0.6033	0.5073	0.5718	0.6702	0.6028	0.5993	0.6928	0.7272
2014Q3	0.5607	0.5839	0.5490	0.5851	0.6837	0.6528	0.3341	0.4978	0.6059	0.5005	0.5730	0.6802	0.6068	0.6000	0.6837	0.7265
2014Q4	0.5754	0.5630	0.5361	0.5803	0.6875	0.6749	0.3234	0.5054	0.6140	0.5096	0.5827	0.7210	0.6090	0.6114	0.6912	0.7243
2015Q1	0.5746	0.5446	0.5123	0.5641	0.6807	0.6741	0.3144	0.4843	0.6662	0.5101	0.5862	0.7300	0.6050	0.6039	0.6859	0.7191
2015Q2	0.5809	0.5670	0.5100	0.5834	0.6780	0.6850	0.3408	0.5066	0.6837	0.5149	0.6019	0.7406	0.6128	0.6123	0.7012	0.7246
2015Q3	0.5853	0.5656	0.5090	0.5831	0.6902	0.6851	0.3362	0.5079	0.6757	0.5342	0.6067	0.7278	0.6133	0.6223	0.6965	0.7314
2015Q4	0.5910	0.5839	0.5021	0.5975	0.6133	0.6893	0.3527	0.5210	0.6477	0.5359	0.6123	0.7438	0.6189	0.6302	0.7038	0.7385
2016Q1	0.5922	0.5687	0.5315	0.5881	0.6237	0.6915	0.3421	0.5144	0.6339	0.5376	0.6200	0.7197	0.6205	0.6307	0.7135	0.7254
2016Q2	0.5939	0.5693	0.5506	0.5804	0.6256	0.6886	0.3389	0.5066	0.6240	0.5267	0.6203	0.7328	0.6116	0.6371	0.7118	0.7285
2016Q3	0.5960	0.5765	0.5514	0.5813	0.6234	0.6882	0.3406	0.4963	0.6101	0.5289	0.6227	0.7261	0.5935	0.6409	0.7211	0.7373
2016Q4	0.6003	0.5756	0.5427	0.5929	0.6323	0.6935	0.3732	0.5096	0.6046	0.5458	0.6347	0.7492	0.5877	0.6537	0.7327	0.7410
2017Q1	0.6099	0.5888	0.5356	0.5927	0.6352	0.7024	0.4378	0.5122	0.5926	0.5386	0.6427	0.7399	0.6034	0.6987	0.7388	0.7396

Table 1.6 Loan to deposit ratio. *Source* Authors' elaboration on data from the ECB Statistical Data Warehouse

Time/ Country	Austria	Belgium	Cyprus	Germany	Estonia	Spain	Finland	France	Greece	Ireland	Italy	Lithuania	Luxembourg	Portugal	Slovenia	Slovakia
2006Q1		0.86	1.11	1.08	1.54	1.13	1.37	1.15	0.94	1.08	1.32	1.26	0.88	1.17	0.87	
2006Q2		0.86	1.12	1.06	1.58	1.16	1.38	1.15	0.92	1.09	1.31	1.28	0.87	1.16	0.86	
2006Q3		0.88	1.13	1.06	1.56	1.16	1.36	1.17	0.95	1.11	1.31	1.24	0.86	1.23	0.88	
2006Q4		0.86	1.13	1.04	1.56	1.15	1.37	1.17	0.93	1.14	1.30	1.22	0.85	1.22	0.89	
2007Q1		0.89	1.07	1.04	1.61	1.15	1.40	1.18	0.94	1.17	1.29	1.27	0.85	1.24	0.88	
2007Q2		0.92	1.12	1.04	1.71	1.16	1.47	1.18	0.96	1.15	1.28	1.35	0.84	1.26	0.91	
2007Q3		0.95	1.06	1.03	1.78	1.16	1.45	1.19	0.97	1.19	1.30	1.42	0.85	1.26	0.93	
2007Q4		0.95	1.08	1.02	1.82	1.12	1.44	1.19	0.95	1.14	1.28	1.43	0.86	1.24	0.92	
2008Q1		0.96	1.11	1.02	1.80	1.13	1.36	1.18	0.96	1.19	1.30	1.45	0.86	1.24	0.92	
2008Q2		0.95	1.10	1.02	1.78	1.11	1.36	1.19	0.91	1.14	1.29	1.50	0.89	1.24	0.93	
2008Q3		0.93	0.99	1.02	1.79	1.10	1.35	1.19	0.91	1.09	1.27	1.49	0.90	1.21	0.94	
2008Q4	1.06	0.86	0.88	1.01	1.82	1.05	1.40	1.13	0.84	0.96	1.25	1.57	0.86	1.15	0.94	
2009Q1	1.07	0.83	0.81	1.02	1.78	1.04	1.42	1.15	0.80	0.88	1.25	1.54	0.89	1.15	0.94	0.96
2009Q2	1.09	0.88	0.78	1.02	1.74	1.03	1.43	1.14	0.79	0.87	1.26	1.50	0.85	1.17	0.93	0.89
2009Q3	1.11	0.89	0.77	1.02	1.68	1.03	1.41	1.14	0.80	0.92	1.25	1.47	0.86	1.15	0.96	0.87
2009Q4	1.10	0.86	0.81	1.01	1.59	1.01	1.44	1.13	0.80	0.91	1.24	1.39	0.83	1.15	0.96	0.86
2010Q1	1.10	0.85	0.81	1.02	1.59	1.02	1.42	1.15	0.77	0.92	1.23	1.33	0.84	1.16	0.97	0.85
2010Q2	1.12	0.86	0.78	1.03	1.53	1.01	1.60	1.15	0.95	0.85	1.16	1.32	0.90	1.07	1.00	0.85
2010Q3	1.11	0.89	0.88	1.04	1.48	1.02	1.45	1.15	0.93	0.83	1.17	1.32	0.89	1.05	1.01	0.83
2010Q4	1.11	0.87	0.86	1.02	1.39	1.02	1.50	1.16	0.93	0.87	1.16	1.32	0.89	1.01	1.02	0.85
2011Q1	1.11	0.87	0.89	1.02	1.33	1.02	1.41	1.16	0.94	0.87	1.19	1.28	0.90	1.01	1.03	0.86
2011Q2	1.10	0.84	0.99	1.01	1.29	1.01	1.46	1.15	0.92	0.89	1.19	1.24	0.90	0.98	1.03	0.89
2011Q3	1.12	0.85	0.94	1.04	1.25	1.00	1.66	1.11	0.92	0.91	1.16	1.25	0.91	0.97	1.04	0.89
2011Q4	1.12	0.82	0.99	1.03	1.26	0.99	1.79	1.11	0.90	0.89	1.13	1.28	0.93	0.95	1.01	0.92
2012Q1	1.11	0.81	1.08	1.06	1.25	0.95	1.82	1.11	0.87	0.86	1.09	1.22	0.96	0.92	1.01	0.91
2012Q2	1.09	0.80	1.02	1.06	1.23	0.93	1.78	1.11	0.86	0.86	1.08	1.20	0.96	0.94	1.01	0.90
2012Q3	1.10	0.78	1.06	1.05	1.19	0.95	1.73	1.12	0.84	0.85	1.07	1.20	0.93	0.95	1.01	0.89
2012Q4	1.10	0.77	1.11	1.03	1.27	0.92	1.73	1.11	0.84	0.87	1.07	1.22	0.91	0.95	1.01	0.89
2013Q1	1.10	0.79	1.25	1.02	1.24	0.90	1.53	1.11	0.89	0.89	1.05	1.21	0.90	0.95	1.00	0.88
2013Q2	1.10	0.78	1.23	1.01	1.22	0.88	1.48	1.10	0.91	0.90	1.03	1.20	0.88	0.93	1.01	0.90
2013Q3	1.09	0.78	1.19	1.01	1.21	0.88	1.45	1.11	0.93	0.90	1.04	1.19	0.87	0.91	1.01	0.90
2013Q4	1.08	0.76	1.22	0.99	1.22	0.89	1.44	1.10	0.92	0.90	1.03	1.19	0.87	0.91	1.01	0.91
2014Q1	1.09	0.76	1.23	0.98	1.19	0.87	1.42	1.10	0.94	0.91	1.04	1.15	0.85	0.92	1.00	0.91
2014Q2	1.08	0.77	1.24	0.97	1.13	0.87	1.43	1.09	1.00	0.91	1.04	1.16	0.84	0.92	1.00	0.93

(continued)

Table 1.6 (continued)

Time/ Country	Austria	Belgium	Cyprus	Germany	Estonia	Spain	Finland	France	Greece	Ireland	Italy	Lithuania	Luxembourg	Portugal	Slovenia	Slovakia
2014Q3	1.07	0.77	1.30	0.98	1.12	0.86	1.40	1.10	0.99	0.89	1.04	1.15	0.83	0.92	1.00	0.93
2014Q4	1.05	0.77	1.33	0.97	1.26	0.86	1.46	1.09	0.97	0.87	1.03	1.16	0.82	0.90	0.96	0.93
2015Q1	1.05	0.82	1.40	0.98	1.13	0.86	1.42	1.08	0.89	0.85	1.02	0.99	0.82	0.91	0.96	0.94
2015Q2	1.06	0.83	1.43	0.98	1.21	0.86	1.42	1.08	0.86	0.88	1.02	1.06	0.80	0.91	0.94	0.93
2015Q3	1.06	0.84	1.45	0.98	1.21	0.86	1.45	1.08	0.86	0.89	1.01	1.08	0.83	0.90	0.94	0.93
2015Q4	1.05	0.83	1.52	0.98	1.49	0.86	1.44	1.08	0.89	0.88	1.01	1.11	0.86	0.89	0.93	0.92
2016Q1	1.05	0.85	1.43	1.00	1.38	0.85	1.53	1.09	0.91	0.87	1.00	1.09	0.87	0.89	0.91	0.95
2016Q2	1.05	0.85	1.37	1.00	1.37	0.85	1.58	1.09	0.94	0.89	0.99	1.09	0.86	0.88	0.91	0.93
2016Q3	1.05	0.85	1.37	1.02	1.43	0.85	1.67	1.11	0.97	0.90	0.99	1.09	0.89	0.88	0.90	0.93
2016Q4	1.05	0.88	1.40	1.02	1.40	0.87	1.53	1.12	0.98	0.88	0.98	1.06	0.93	0.86	0.92	0.95
2017Q1	1.03	0.89	1.41	1.03	1.40	0.85	1.73	1.11	1.01	0.92	0.97	1.08	0.91	0.87	0.92	0.93

remarkable in many countries. The ratio is now below (or near) 100% in the majority of the banking systems. However, this data should be taken cautiously: indeed, a ratio below 100% could indicate an efficient balance sheet structure, in which deposits are sufficient to fund loans. But this condition could also conceal a credit crunch phenomenon in the period investigated or, put it another way, a widespread change in banks' business models. Figure 1.4 and Table 1.7 can help to better understand the situation.

Indeed, In Fig. 1.4 we present the evolution of the Loan-to-Deposit ratio in four major countries. The (negative) trend characterizing this ratio for Italy and Spain—two countries strongly hit by the credit crunch in the aftermath of the financial crisis—is more pronounced and very similar (even if the starting point is different). In France and in Germany, instead, the decline in the ratio is less evident. In Germany, probably due to a stronger GDP growth rate in the last few years, the ratio starts to increase again from 2014:Q4.

In Table 1.7, one can appreciate the share of loans to total assets. Here again, we observe a totally different situation between Italy and Spain on the one hand, and Germany and France on the other. For the first two,

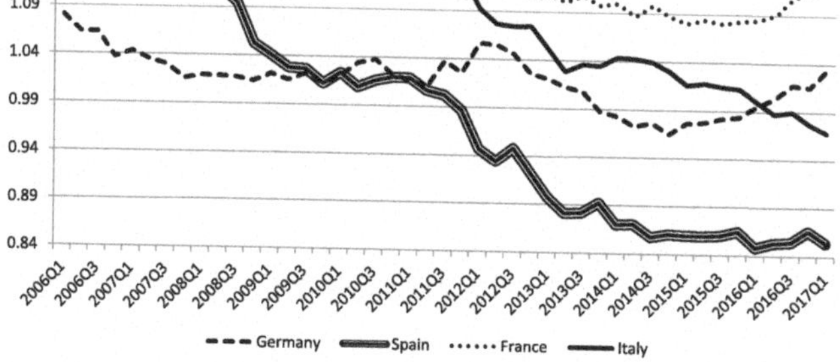

Fig. 1.4 Loan-to-deposit ratio, selected countries. *Source* Authors' elaboration on data from the ECB Statistical Data Warehouse

Table 1.7 Loans to total assets. *Source* Authors' elaboration on data from the ECB Statistical Data Warehouse

Time/ Country	Austria	Belgium	Cyprus	Germany	Estonia	Spain	Finland	France	Greece	Ireland	Italy	Lithuania	Luxembourg	Portugal	Slovenia	Slovakia
2006Q1		0.4821	0.5932	0.6139	0.7754	0.7260	0.5703	0.5402	0.6048	0.4859	0.6921	0.7952	0.4877	0.7083	0.6716	
2006Q2		0.4893	0.6039	0.6093	0.8018	0.7410	0.5783	0.5516	0.5988	0.4854	0.6983	0.8024	0.4877	0.7036	0.6769	
2006Q3		0.4936	0.5943	0.6058	0.8312	0.7454	0.5900	0.5409	0.6038	0.4875	0.7041	0.7982	0.4798	0.7155	0.6830	
2006Q4		0.4881	0.5696	0.5977	0.8292	0.7458	0.5791	0.5382	0.5975	0.4813	0.7002	0.7842	0.4706	0.7110	0.6953	
2007Q1		0.4981	0.5517	0.5952	0.8281	0.7402	0.5730	0.5265	0.6050	0.4723	0.6851	0.7975	0.4859	0.7172	0.6748	
2007Q2		0.4879	0.5657	0.5909	0.7950	0.7395	0.5928	0.5240	0.6149	0.4577	0.6797	0.8059	0.4813	0.7169	0.6849	
2007Q3		0.4998	0.5465	0.5909	0.8078	0.7374	0.5769	0.5358	0.6177	0.4576	0.6887	0.8092	0.4889	0.7245	0.7007	
2007Q4		0.5068	0.5636	0.5962	0.8255	0.7266	0.5799	0.5433	0.6148	0.4586	0.6981	0.8150	0.4938	0.7215	0.7032	
2008Q1		0.5202	0.5699	0.5958	0.8337	0.7199	0.5405	0.5392	0.6225	0.4480	0.6948	0.8138	0.5137	0.7228	0.7131	
2008Q2		0.4973	0.5754	0.5980	0.8413	0.7138	0.5282	0.5456	0.6038	0.4488	0.6891	0.8388	0.5305	0.7144	0.7209	
2008Q3		0.5201	0.5643	0.5947	0.8472	0.7088	0.5325	0.5463	0.6049	0.4611	0.6862	0.8349	0.5243	0.7104	0.7322	
2008Q4	0.5924	0.4648	0.5562	0.6035	0.8545	0.6890	0.4930	0.5359	0.5897	0.4701	0.6813	0.8375	0.5159	0.6903	0.7362	0.7373
2009Q1	0.5954	0.4504	0.5381	0.6039	0.8596	0.6705	0.4842	0.5420	0.5777	0.4647	0.6700	0.8199	0.5157	0.6680	0.7309	0.6700
2009Q2	0.5970	0.4953	0.5317	0.6097	0.8563	0.6676	0.5091	0.5361	0.5818	0.4612	0.6727	0.8114	0.5117	0.6730	0.7315	0.6606
2009Q3	0.5951	0.4952	0.5185	0.6121	0.8331	0.6649	0.4982	0.5335	0.5753	0.4622	0.6679	0.7914	0.5065	0.6575	0.7261	0.6453
2009Q4	0.5965	0.4710	0.5370	0.6121	0.8196	0.6624	0.5070	0.5449	0.5800	0.4580	0.5738	0.7793	0.5014	0.6479	0.7305	0.6480
2010Q1	0.5882	0.4617	0.5387	0.6121	0.8236	0.6567	0.4878	0.5376	0.5670	0.4564	0.6633	0.7696	0.4912	0.6346	0.7284	0.6307
2010Q2	0.5999	0.4636	0.5499	0.6183	0.8145	0.6534	0.4807	0.5337	0.6524	0.4369	0.6470	0.7657	0.5130	0.6161	0.7306	0.6216
2010Q3	0.5925	0.4638	0.5788	0.6232	0.7961	0.6501	0.4384	0.5220	0.6562	0.4568	0.6440	0.7719	0.5137	0.6074	0.7298	0.6332
2010Q4	0.5950	0.4825	0.5559	0.5557	0.7839	0.6559	0.4576	0.5357	0.6591	0.5091	0.6453	0.7716	0.5235	0.6015	0.7352	0.6452
2011Q1	0.6015	0.4793	0.5549	0.5710	0.7732	0.6560	0.4371	0.5597	0.6515	0.5172	0.6534	0.7672	0.5351	0.6010	0.7336	0.6499
2011Q2	0.6054	0.4772	0.5936	0.5730	0.7582	0.6423	0.4497	0.5585	0.6572	0.5081	0.6501	0.7467	0.5368	0.5880	0.7358	0.6552
2011Q3	0.6100	0.4717	0.5818	0.5559	0.7715	0.6275	0.4306	0.5324	0.6501	0.5032	0.6339	0.7492	0.5392	0.5784	0.7404	0.6633
2011Q4	0.6041	0.4580	0.5968	0.5595	0.7793	0.6196	0.4522	0.5466	0.6464	0.4924	0.6169	0.7816	0.5444	0.5656	0.7317	0.6626
2012Q1	0.6121	0.4629	0.6240	0.5749	0.7784	0.6095	0.4688	0.5412	0.6584	0.4758	0.5979	0.7516	0.5559	0.5551	0.7323	0.6580
2012Q2	0.6100	0.4463	0.6225	0.5697	0.7924	0.6020	0.4657	0.5378	0.6310	0.4752	0.5930	0.7608	0.5540	0.5514	0.7338	0.6542
2012Q3	0.6094	0.4397	0.6327	0.5651	0.7744	0.6029	0.4667	0.5375	0.6137	0.4643	0.5923	0.7699	0.5432	0.5501	0.7333	0.6534
2012Q4	0.6028	0.4520	0.6385	0.5670	0.8265	0.5861	0.5074	0.5679	0.6023	0.4657	0.5864	0.7851	0.5315	0.5510	0.7271	0.6547
2013Q1	0.6033	0.4591	0.6842	0.5718	0.8212	0.5720	0.4874	0.5374	0.6039	0.4617	0.5850	0.7747	0.5280	0.5484	0.7329	0.6620
2013Q2	0.6044	0.4736	0.6881	0.5847	0.8180	0.5652	0.5045	0.5430	0.5973	0.4668	0.5820	0.7752	0.5249	0.5434	0.7364	0.6622
2013Q3	0.6064	0.4588	0.6983	0.5901	0.8151	0.5705	0.4999	0.5504	0.6065	0.4672	0.5855	0.7743	0.5224	0.5432	0.7340	0.6646
2013Q4	0.6057	0.4604	0.7077	0.5886	0.8213	0.5809	0.5049	0.5674	0.6045	0.4672	0.5897	0.7843	0.5201	0.5503	0.6977	0.6734
2014Q1	0.6013	0.4594	0.7009	0.5871	0.8032	0.5700	0.5003	0.5648	0.5971	0.4781	0.5951	0.7634	0.5041	0.5503	0.6941	0.6694
2014Q2	0.6022	0.4578	0.7022	0.5800	0.7635	0.5698	0.4948	0.5609	0.6006	0.4628	0.5963	0.7773	0.5053	0.5523	0.6909	0.6717

(continued)

Table 1.7 (continued)

Time/ Country	Austria	Belgium	Cyprus	Germany	Estonia	Spain	Finland	France	Greece	Ireland	Italy	Lithuania	Luxembourg	Portugal	Slovenia	Slovakia
2014Q3	0.6026	0.4511	0.7123	0.5714	0.7692	0.5600	0.4689	0.5468	0.5986	0.4444	0.5957	0.7800	0 5010	0.5493	0.6830	0.6740
2014Q4	0.6036	0.4353	0.7150	0.5601	0.8661	0.5810	0.4737	0.5494	0.5931	0.4435	0.6004	0.8376	0.5009	0.5517	0.6610	0.6710
2015Q1	0.6019	0.4458	0.7184	0.5510	0.7699	0.5796	0.4460	0.5232	0.5922	0.4355	0.5957	0.7215	0.4970	0.5524	0.6566	0.6772
2015Q2	0.6136	0.4721	0.7303	0.5705	0.8176	0.5887	0.4832	0.5494	0.5899	0.4507	0.6128	0.7855	0.4928	0.5552	0.6557	0.6716
2015Q3	0.6177	0.4772	0.7368	0.5726	0.8361	0.5892	0.4869	0.5486	0.5836	0.4739	0.6158	0.7859	0.5073	0.5604	0.6535	0.6770
2015Q4	0.6230	0.4863	0.7632	0.5877	0.9136	0.5960	0.5073	0.5645	0.5782	0.4698	0.6202	0.8258	0.5295	0.5635	0.6513	0.6792
2016Q1	0.6226	0.4814	0.7586	0.5856	0.8636	0.5867	0.5220	0.5582	0.5756	0.4664	0.6200	0.7862	0.5381	0.5619	0.6517	0.6864
2016Q2	0.6207	0.4832	0.7544	0.5826	0.8592	0.5876	0.5371	0.5524	0.5893	0.4668	0.6126	0.7953	0.5287	0.5607	0.6500	0.6795
2016Q3	0.6282	0.4929	0.7540	0.5918	0.8910	0.5880	0.5701	0.5496	0.5901	0.4750	0.6166	0.7926	0.5291	0.5623	0.6484	0.6848
2016Q4	0.6291	0.5091	0.7582	0.6022	0.8843	0.6007	0.5711	0.5699	0.5951	0.4821	0.6204	0.7951	0.5455	0.5654	0.6722	0.7007
2017Q1	0.6293	0.5262	0.7574	0.6130	0.8906	0.5999	0.7584	0.5710	0.6007	0.4931	0.6220	0.7971	0.5479	0.6092	0.6800	0.6877

we find that the ratio starts to decrease dramatically from the last quarter of 2006 until at least the last quarter of 2012. In Italy, the reduction amounts approximately to 10% points (from 68.51 to 58.64%), whereas in Spain the difference is even higher and about 15% points. In contrast, in Germany and France, the ratio tends to remain more stable.

1.4 Conclusions

Last decade has been characterized by remarkable events (i.e. two major financial crises) that have heavily affected the stability of the financial systems and the European economy. Indeed, the implications generated by the crises on the real economy (low GDP growth, high levels of non-performing loans, extraordinary monetary policy measures, low interest rates and so on), along with the important regulatory changes affecting banks, have surely had an impact on the behaviour of European banks in regard to their approach towards funding.

The common thinking arising from the academic literature—also corroborated by our analysis of aggregated data drawn from the European Central Bank Data Warehouse—is that, at least for the largest European economies, retail deposits have acquired an increasing importance in terms of main funding instrument available to the credit institutions. Indeed, banks have progressively replaced wholesale funding (that was strongly used before the Global Financial Crisis), in favour of deposits. Moreover, our analysis has also highlighted a decline in the volume of bonds issued by the financial institutions over the last few years.

We further explore this issue in the following chapter, where we provide a specific focus on the importance of bonds within the funding strategies adopted by the Italian banks during the last 10 years.

References

Agur, I., 2013. Wholesale bank funding, capital requirements and credit rationing. Journal of Financial Stability 9, 38–45.

Basel Committee on Banking Supervision, 2014a. Basel III leverage ratio framework and disclosure requirements. Bank for International Settlements. Basel (Switzerland).

Basel Committee on Banking Supervision, 2014b. Liquidity coverage ratio disclosure. Bank for International Settlements. Basel (Switzerland).

Basel Committee on Banking Supervision, 2014c. Basel III: The net stable funding ratio. Bank for International Settlements. Basel (Switzerland).

Berger, A., DeYoung, R., Flannery, M., Lee, D. Öztekin, Ö., 2008. How do large banking organizations manage their capital ratios? Journal of Financial Services Research 34, 123–149.

CGFS, 2010. Funding patterns and liquidity management of internationally active banks. Committee on the Global Financial System Papers No. 39.

ECB, 2009. EU Banks' funding structures and policies. European Central Bank, Frankfurt (Germany).

ECB, 2012. Changes in bank financing patterns. European Central Bank, Frankfurt (Germany).

ECB, 2016. Recent developments in the composition and cost of bank funding in the euro area. Economic Bulletin 1, 26–45.

Evanoff, D.D., Jagtiani, J.A., Nakata, T., 2011. Enhancing market discipline in banking: The role of subordinated debt in financial regulatory reform. Journal of Economics and Business 63(1), 1–22.

Flannery, M., 1994. Debt maturity and the deadweight cost of leverage: Optimally financing banking firms. American Economic Review 84(1), 320–331.

Frank, M.Z., Goyal, V.K., 2009. Capital structure decisions: Which factors are reliably important? Financial management 38(1), 1–37.

Gambacorta, L., van Rixtel, A., Schiaffi, S., 2017. Changing business models in international bank funding. BIS Working Papers No. 614.

Gropp, R., Heider, F., 2009. The determinants of bank capital structure. European Central Bank Working Paper Series No. 1096.

Le Leslé, V., 2012. Bank debt in Europe: "Are funding models broken?". IMF Working Paper No. 12/299.

Mendicino, C., Nokolov, K., Suarez, J., 2017. Equity versus bail-in debt in banking: Am agency perspective. ESRB Working Paper Series No. 50.

Mishkin, F., 2000. The economics of money, banking and financial markets. Pearson education.

Van Rixtel, A., Gasperini, G., 2013. Financial crises and bank funding: Recent experience in the euro area. BIS Working Papers No. 406.

Van Rixtel, A., Gonzalez, L.R., Yang, J., 2015. The determinants of long-term debt issuance by European banks: Evidence of two crises. BIS Working Papers No. 513.

2

The Funding Strategies of Italian Banks: The Importance of Bonds

Abstract The analysis of the funding strategies adopted by the Italian banks over the last ten years confirms the trends observed for the banks operating in the major European countries. Indeed, since late 2012 deposits have been steadily growing, the weight of bonds, compared to the liabilities, has sharply declined. We find that, after a peak of 11% reached in 2011, at the end of 2016 the share of households' wealth invested in banks' bonds was around 3.3% only. Furthermore, until 2007 banks were used to place the majority of their bonds to households. After a steady decline throughout the years, at the end of 2016 only 25% of bank bonds appeared to be in retail investors' portfolios. Overall, this underscores the key role played by the banks in guiding households' investments decisions.

Keywords Funding strategies · Deposits · Bonds · Opacity · MiFID

F. Crespi and D. V. Mascia, *Bank Funding Strategies*, Palgrave Macmillan Studies in Banking and Financial Institutions, https://doi.org/10.1007/978-3-319-69413-9_2

2.1 Introduction

The analysis of the Italian banks' funding strategies and, in particular, the investigation about the use of bonds as a source of long-term financing, is interesting (from a theoretical point view) for different reasons.

First of all, historically the Italian financial system is a bank-oriented one, embedded in an economic system in which unlisted small- and medium-sized enterprises (SMEs) play a major role. Consequently, the financial intermediation and the maturity transformation function operated by banks constitute the basic channel to transfer savings to investments. On the other hand, the importance of financial markets (stock exchange in particular) has always been secondary for the funding of SMEs.[1] More recently, new forms of intermediation, such as minibonds, crowdfunding, peer-to-peer lending and PIR[2] appeared as alternative ways for SMEs to raise money, but they only represent a limited part of the financial intermediation.

In addition, Italian households (traditionally 'addicted' to savings, even if the saving ratio on disposable income has significantly decreased after the crisis)[3] have generally preferred to invest their savings in bank deposits or bonds issued by financial intermediaries. In particular, until at least 2012, bonds were among the main sources of external funding for Italian banks and one of the most important financial assets held by Italian households. As reported by Coletta and Santioni (2016), the percentage of bonds over total liabilities of Italian banks reached a peak

[1]At the end of 2016, only 387 companies were listed in the Italian stock exchange, of which 77 in the Alternative Investment Market (AIM), a special trading venue dedicated to SMEs. The total market capitalization was 525,050 millions of Euro, that is 31.8% of the GPD. About 80% of this capitalization refers to the 40 largest companies, all of them belonging to the FTSE MIB Index (which is the main index of the Italian stock exchange).

[2]Piani Individuali di Risparmio (individual savings accounts) were introduced at the beginning of 2017 as a new instrument to improve the financing of SMEs. Households investing in PIR (that are usually represented by specialized mutual funds) are granted a total tax exemption if they maintain their investments for 5 years. The main feature of a PIR is that it must necessarily invest a minimum percentage (21%) in instruments (bonds and equity) issued by companies that are not included in the FTSE MIB Index.

[3]For an international comparison, see https://data.oecd.org/hha/household-savings.htm#indicator-chart.

in that year (25%), while the share of bank bonds on Italian households' financial wealth (about 11%) was by far the highest among major industrialized economies. Then, a dramatic drop in the issuance of bonds by Italian banks occurred, while households turned their attention to short-term bank deposits and mutual funds.

Second, the Italian banking system has undergone a dramatic restructuring in the last decade, due to the strong impact of the financial crisis (2007–2009) and the Euro area crisis (2010–2012). As we are going to describe in Chap. 4, this reorganization produced a sort of 'ante litteram' *bail-in* of four banks in November 2015, the disappearance of two historical credit cooperatives operating in the most industrialized part of the country and, finally, the nationalization of the oldest bank in the world, Monte dei Paschi di Siena (founded in 1472).

Given the structure of the banking system and the transformation occurred in the last few years, along with the propensity of Italian households to mainly allocate their savings into bank deposits and bank bonds, it is not inappropriate to say that the examination of Italian banks' funding strategies represents an interesting study of the changing conditions after the crisis.

In this chapter, we thus investigate the main topics and issues regarding the Italian banking system and, through the use of aggregated data, we provide empirical evidence about the evolution of the credit institutions' funding choices.

2.2 The Italian Banking System: An Overview

It is a well-known fact that Italy is characterized by a bank-oriented financial system. Indeed, the majority of funding sources for large companies and SMEs comes from traditional bank products, such as credit lines, trade credit in the form of receivable discounts, factoring, mortgages and leasing. Other types of financing, such as venture capital and private equity, commercial papers or bond issuing, and the public placement of shares are not common among Italian SMEs, even though such tools are available (see, for instance, Accornero et al. 2015).

The total bank credit for industrial and family businesses amounted to 862,150 millions of Euro in March 2017 (roughly 51% of the GDP) according to the Statistical Bulletin of the Bank of Italy (see Bank of Italy 2017a). Yet, after the 2011 sovereign debt crisis, we witnessed a tightening of bank lending standards and a reduction in bank credit offered to SMEs until at least mid-2015. Better conditions started to appear in the third quarter of last year, according to the European Central Bank (ECB 2016).

Moreover, Italian households have generally preferred to invest their savings in bank deposits or bonds issued by financial intermediaries. Notably, the net financial wealth of Italian households was estimated (by the Bank of Italy) in 3,239 billions of Euro (194% of the GDP) at the end of 2016.[4] The financial resources invested in Italian banks' deposits amount to 1,112,452 millions of Euro, while those invested in Italian banks' bonds have strongly decreased in the last few years and amount now to 136,407 millions of Euro.

To better understand the structure and the size of the Italian banking system, we focus on the main aspects that have reshaped it in the last few years. Broadly speaking, these aspects include: (i) a long-lasting process of concentration through mergers and acquisitions (M&As); (ii) the consequences of the financial crises in terms of reduction of profitability and redefinition of banks' business models; and (iii) a shift in banks' funding strategies away from bonds issuance.

2.2.1 Number of Credit Institutions and Changes in the Distribution Channels

At the end of 2016, accordingly to the Annual Report edited by the Bank of Italy (see Bank of Italy 2017b), 70 banking groups (which included 129 single banks), 393 stand-alone banks and 82 subsidiaries/

[4]Net financial wealth is the difference between gross financial wealth (4,168,002 millions of Euro) and financial liabilities (928,230 millions of Euro).

branches of foreign banks, for a total of 604 institutions (–39 from 2015), were operating in Italy. Fourteen banking groups are classified as 'significant' by the Single Supervisory Mechanism (SSM), and their assets represent 74% of the entire system's total assets.

Notwithstanding a process of concentration that is eroding year by year the number of operating institutions, the Italian banking system yet remains essentially fragmented. The most populated category of stand-alone banks is represented by cooperative banks (335). However, following the introduction of a new regulation in 2016, cooperative banks will be forced to enter a banking group in order to continue to operate as cooperatives. Estimates show that, in the near future, almost all the cooperative banks will be enclosed in just two or three banking groups. Another category of banks is 'Banche Popolari' (the Italian version of the German 'Volksbanken'): these banks historically operated as cooperatives as well, but in 2016 they have been forced by law to turn into limited companies when their total assets exceed 8 billions of Euro. Therefore, a trend of aggregation is also underway in this category.[5]

An interesting trend characterizing the structure of the banking system concerns the reorganization of the distribution channels, mainly caused by the accelerating widespread use of new technologies and by the above-mentioned concentration process among banks. The number of 'brick and mortar' bank offices has sharply declined since 2007 (–4,197 units). Nevertheless, in 2015, the number of bank offices every 10,000 inhabitants in Italy was higher than the European average (but lower than Spain and France). Innovative distribution channels (e.g. smartphone and web) are increasing in terms of importance: in 2016, about 62% of households were able to access their bank accounts through digital channels.[6]

---

[5]For example, two of the largest 'Banche Popolari', namely Banco Popolare and BPM, merged in 2016.

[6]The reshaping of the distribution channels is creating a dramatic drop of jobs in the banking industry.

2.2.2 The Financial Crisis and the Euro Area Debt Crisis: Main Effects

Oddly enough, the Italian banking system appeared more resilient than others, at the dawn of the financial crisis. Indeed, the business model of Italian banks was mainly focused on retail deposits and retail loans; few banks were engaged in investment banking activities; asset-backed securities were not so widespread in banks' portfolio. It was indeed the subsequent deterioration of the economic conditions (Italian GDP decreased by 7% from 2012 to 2017) that worsened the performance and the stability of Italian banks.

In particular, starting from 2008 and till 2015, we observed a dramatic increase of non-performing loans (NPLs, that is bad loans and other past due and substandard loans) in banks' balance sheets. Gross bad loans alone reached an abnormal level of 201,028 millions of Euro in November 2015 (i.e. much more than 10% of Italian GDP); at the same time, the net amount (i.e. after devaluation) was 88,832 millions of Euro, or 4.89% of total loans.[7] The situation started to improve in 2016, thanks to monster securitization transactions: in May 2017, net bad loans amounted to 76,501 millions of Euro, or 4.38% of total loans.[8] Moreover, the ratio of new bad loans over total loans has returned close to a pre-crisis level; however, meanwhile, SMEs have been hit by a deep credit crunch phenomenon.

Another implication of the financial crisis was the reduction of banks' profitability, mainly due to the significant decrease affecting interest rate margins. In June 2017, the spread between the average interest rate on loans to households and non-financial companies, and the average interest rate on funding from the same counterparts, reached a minimum level of 181 basis points. For the sake of comparability, note that, at the end of 2007, the same spread was 329 basis points.

[7]The difference between gross and net amounts in bad loans was registered as losses in banks' income statements.

[8]Data were collected from ABI Monthly Outlook. ABI is the Association of Italian banks. In 2015, the amount of total (gross) NPLs was over 360 billion of Euro, or 18% of total assets; in other words, almost one loan out of five was in trouble.

An interesting analysis on the profitability and balance sheet repair of Italian banks appeared in an IMF paper written by Jobst and Weber (2016). The authors point out how the high stock of impaired assets and the associated cost of risk due to the need for continued provisioning had dragged down banks' earnings capacity; this, in turn, had limited the build-up of capital buffers and slowed the repair of balance sheets. Moreover, they indicate how operating costs for the Italian banking system overall were marginally higher than the weighted average of EU banks, but strongly higher than EU median; the well-known cost-to-income ratio for the Italian banking system as a whole was indeed 63% at the end of 2015.[9] Then, in 2016 the ratio grew to 73.6%, but that was mainly due to the extraordinary expenses related to the (exit) incentives plans implemented to reduce the number of employees.

In its Annual Report (see Bank of Italy 2017b), the Bank of Italy compares the evolutions of banks' ROE in different European countries between years 2006–2007 and 2015–2016 (the sample consists of 61 major banks). Figure 2.1 shows that the profitability significantly dropped (on average 14%) even if there is an evident heterogeneity. Especially in Italy, the fall is mainly due to decreasing revenues[10] and devaluations (of NPLs).

In Fig. 2.1, indeed, we observe that revenues and devaluations mostly contributed to the reduction of Italian banks' ROE. In contrast, in Germany revenues had a positive impact on ROE, while operating costs, devaluation and leverage negatively affected it.

In order to counterbalance the drop in interest rate margins, and the overall fall of profitability, many Italian banks tried:

1. to overhaul the composition of liabilities in favour of cheaper ones (such as retail deposits or central bank money);

[9]In their paper, Jobst and Weber (2016) try to evaluate how the profitability of Italian banks could recover if economic headwinds and structural hurdles were removed. Even if their analysis is limited to the 15 largest banks, they find that the system is overall profitable, but there exist significant heterogeneities across banks.

[10]Operating costs, on the other hand, contribute positively—probably due to the reorganization process of the distribution channels.

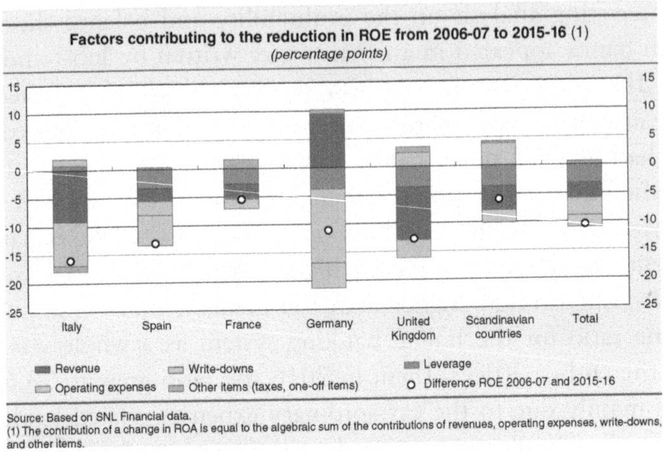

Fig. 2.1 Items contributing to the decrease of ROE between years 2006–2007 and 2015–2016 (percentage points). *Source* Bank of Italy (2017b)

2. to reshape their business model by increasing non-interest revenues, such as commissions for advisory services and placement of asset management products (mutual funds, pension funds, insurance products).

Both these measures (together with other external factors) contributed to the strong reduction in the issuance of bonds.

2.3 The Funding Strategies of Italian Banks: Evidence from Aggregated Data

Similarly to other European financial institutions, the funding structures of Italian banks deeply changed, as well, after the blast of the financial crisis and the Euro area crisis. Overall, according to data from the Bank of Italy, banks reduced wholesale funding in favour of retail deposits and Eurosystem funding.

Notably, during the Euro crisis period, and later on, the growth of funding was mainly sustained by the Eurosystem refinancing operations: at the end of 2016, this form of financing represented 8.7% of the total funding. Moreover, between 2011 and 2012 we observed a strong decrease of non-residents deposits. In addition, the growth of funding via bonds issuances to retail and institutional investors considerably declined since 2012. These trends (i.e. more retail deposits and Eurosystem funding, versus less bonds issuances) have strongly reduced the average maturity of liabilities. Indeed, the total amount of short-term deposits collected from households was about 948 billions of Euro in 2017:Q1, of which 590 in checking accounts. In June 2017, the total amount of short-term deposits from resident depositors (household and others) reached the amount of 1,394 billions of Euro.

The share of loans not financed by retail funding keeps diminishing: at the end of 2016, the gap was 6.1%, or 15 percentage points lower than the level of 2008. The fall of the funding gap is not only due to the constant increase of retail deposits, but also to the persistent weak credit growth. Interestingly, the current average funding cost for Italian banks, 0.39%, has reached a historically minimum level. Indeed, thanks to ECB unprecedented monetary stimulus that followed the famous Draghi's '*whatever it takes*' speech, the negative impact of the sovereign debt crisis on Italian banks' funding costs has disappeared.

Finally, we provide some insights about the evolution of capital components since 2007. Even if in 2016 the capital components have been influenced by the negative economic results of some major groups—so that the CET1 ratio decreased by 80 basis points to a level of 11.5% for the entire system—we observed a constant improvement throughout the post-crises years. More specifically, the CET1 increased by approximately 30%, compared to the level registered in 2007. Meanwhile, a strong reduction in risk weighted assets (RWAs) occurred (almost—25%).[11] After the strong capital injection implemented by UniCredit at the beginning of 2017 (13 billions of Euro),[12] the average level of CET1 ratio in Italy has returned over 12%.

[11]Italian banks raised 60 billions of Euro in equity instruments since 2007. On the other hand, the fall of RWAs is the effect of three main elements: (i) the adoption of internal rating-based models, for measuring credit risk, by the major players; (ii) the reshaping of portfolios in favour of less risky assets; and (iii) the reduction of defaulted exposures through devaluation.

[12]The recapitalization occurred at UniCredit basically followed a strong devaluation of impaired loans.

To better understand the dynamics of different funding instruments in Italian banks' balance sheets (along with some items from the assets side), we present and analyse the following data, which have been gathered from the Statistical Database ('Base Dati Statistica', BDS) available at Bank of Italy,[13] the Italian Central Bank. Interestingly, such database offers an outstanding coverage of more than 18 years, which allows for comparability of the data throughout a very wide time frame. For the purpose of our study, we focus on the monthly time series obtained by aggregating data from resident banks' balance sheets. Notably, we focus on some categories of the assets (coded as BISIB0100) and liabilities (coded as BISIB0200).

Specifically, from the assets side, we collect data regarding 'loans to residents' and 'total assets' that are useful to measure the dimensions of the Italian banking industry. From the liabilities side, instead, we collect aggregated data regarding 'deposits from residents', 'bonds issued', 'capital and reserves' and 'total liabilities' (which clearly equals 'total assets' from the left-hand side of the balance sheet). The data are provided in millions of Euro, as outstanding amounts at the end of each period, from January 1999 to June 2017.

Based on the above-mentioned categories, we build—in a similar fashion to Chap. 1—a number of representative statistics for the Italian banking industry. Namely, we generate the loans-to-deposits ratio, to have an idea of the extent to which loans to residents are financed by deposits of residents. Then, we create the loans over total assets ratio to give a picture about the importance of the lending activity within the banking system, throughout the observed period. Furthermore, from the liabilities side, we generate the ratios deposits-to-liabilities, bonds-to-liabilities and others-to-liabilities[14] to assess how important deposits and bonds are for the composition of the bank's liabilities. Finally, we compute equity-to-total assets to roughly show how Italian bankers

[13]The database is available at the following link: http://www.bancaditalia.it/statistiche/basi-dati/bds/index.html.

[14]In this case, we use as denominator total liabilities, which equals total assets minus capital and reserves. "Others" refers to the remaining forms of funding (i.e. everything apart from bonds and deposits from residents).

Fig. 2.2 Loans-to-deposits ratio of Italian banks; January 1999–June 2017. *Source* Authors' elaboration on data from Bank of Italy's Statistical Database

have increasingly complied with the regulatory requirements. The entire data set is available in Appendix A1.

Figure 2.2 shows the dynamics of the loans-to-deposits ratio. The trend is pretty much similar to the one observed in other European countries (see Chap. 1). Indeed, in the years preceding the crisis (i.e. until 30 September 2007), the ratio increased from 1.28 to 1.52—suggesting that the increase in loans to resident borrowers (and the consequent increase in total assets) was not sufficiently covered by the growth of deposits from residents. In absolute numbers, from 31 January 1999 to 30 September 2007, loans boosted from 882,454.32 to 1,919,969.54 millions of Euro (+118%), total asset soared from 1,598,917.87 to 3,033,509.22 millions of Euro (+90%), deposits from residents increased from 687,194.54 to 1,259,262.67 (+83%) and bonds from 251,157.05 to 583,724.97 millions (+132%). It is clear that the credit boom was substantially financed by bonds and other liabilities, that grew from 550,107.75 to 948,277.38 millions (+72%).

In contrast, from 30 September 2007 to 30 June 2017, the loans-to-deposits ratio constantly decreased until reaching the level of 1.04.

However, it is worth noting that, after 30 September 2007 and up to 31 July 2012, the absolute amounts of bonds issuances increased again until a maximum of 966,302.09 millions of Euro (+66% throughout the period). But in the meantime, the growth of deposits was higher than that of loans: indeed, deposits grew by 64% from 30 September

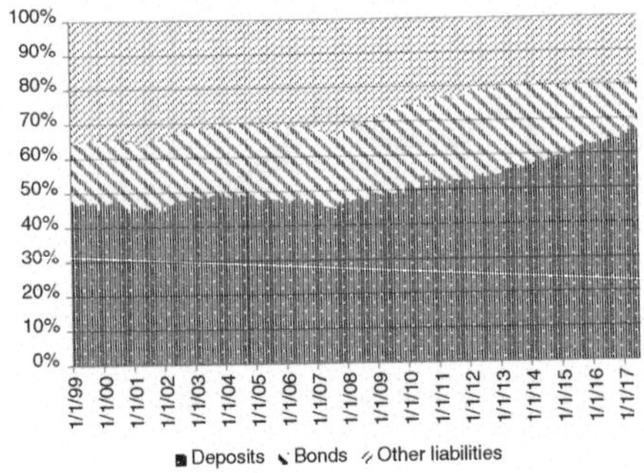

Fig. 2.3 Breakdown of banks' debt, by main balance sheet categories; January 1999–June 2017. *Source* Authors' elaboration on data from Bank of Italy's Statistical Database

2007 until 31 July 2012, while loans increased just about 24% and other liabilities decreased by 12% in the same stretch of time.

Figure 2.3 shows how the funding mix of Italian banks has changed over time. We consider in this figure three broad liabilities categories, namely deposits, bonds and other liabilities—together summing up to the value of total assets minus capital and reserves.

Here again, it is clear that, after the crisis, deposits assumed an increasing role in the funding mix. The ratio of deposits over liabilities, which was 0.45 on 30 September 2007, grew to 0.54 on 31 July 2012 (the date in which bonds reached their maximum level) and again to 0.67 in June 2017. In contrast, the bonds over liabilities ratio, after reaching a 25% share of the liabilities in July 2012[15] (from an original level of 0.17 in 1999), finally fell into 0.15 in June 2017—see Fig. 2.4.

Finally, Fig. 2.5 shows the dynamics of capital and reserves over total assets. The effects of the new capital requirements regulation are evident: since 31 May 2010, after a long period in which the ratio remained nearly constant (between 7% and 8%), a deep increase up to 11.32% was registered in June 2016. Anyway, such an increase represents an apparent improvement in the aggregated banks' capitalization ratio. Indeed, from May 2010 to June 2016, capital and reserves grew

[15]Actually, a maximum level of 0.26 was reached some months before July 2012.

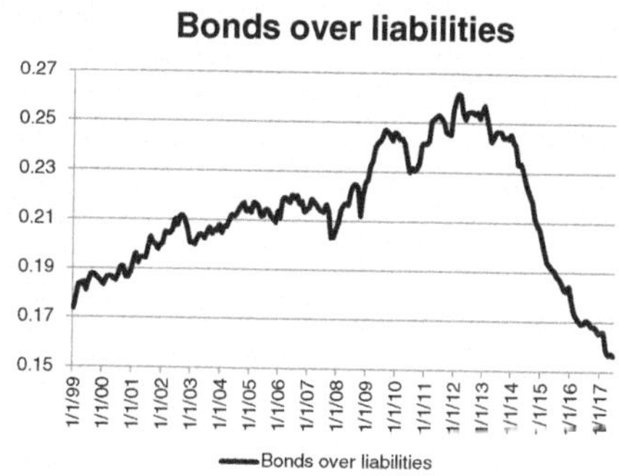

Fig. 2.4 Bonds over liabilities; January 1999–June 2017. *Source* Authors' elaboration on data from Bank of Italy's Statistical Database

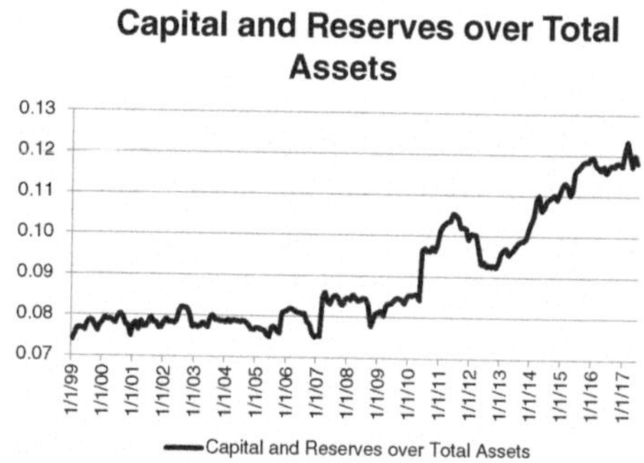

Fig. 2.5 Capital and reserves over total assets; January 1999–June 2017. *Source* Authors' elaboration on data from Bank of Italy's Statistical Database

by 19%, while total assets decreased by 8%. In other words: less business, more capital (which *caeteris paribus* also implies lower ROE).

2.4 Households Investments in Banks' Bonds: A Changed Game

The analysis of the use of bonds as a funding source for banks cannot be untied from the analysis of the investment decisions of Italian households. Compared to other major economies, the volume of banks'

Table 2.1 Italian household financial wealth composition (millions of Euro and percentages). *Source* Bank of Italy Annual Report (2016)

	2016	%
Overall bank deposits	1,143,739	27.40
Bonds:	362,340	8.70
of which		
- Italian Government	131,156	3.10
- Banks	136,407	3.30
Mutual funds	479,980	11.50
Shares and other forms of equity	916,765	22.00
Insurance and pension products	953,033	22.90
Others instruments issued by domestic entities	312,144	7.50
Total	4,168,002	100.00

bonds over the financial wealth of Italian households, as well as the share of banks' bonds directly held by Italian households over the total amount issued, has been traditionally higher. Indeed, direct investment in banks' bond by Italian families dates back to the 1950s.

More recently, as reported first in Grasso et al. (2010), then in Coletta and Santioni (2016), the percentage of households' wealth invested in banks' bonds, which was below 2% in the mid-1990s, reached an 11% maximum level in 2011, then decreasing to 3.3% at the end of 2016.

As pointed out by the Bank of Italy's Annual Report (Bank of Italy 2017b), at the end of 2016, the financial wealth of Italian households invested in banks' bonds was about 136,407 millions of Euro (see Table 2.1). Considering that, at the same date, the total amount of banks' bonds outstanding was 558,028 millions of Euro, a share of 24.44% was indeed in retail investors' hands.

The fast growth of the percentage of banks' bond in households' portfolios in the first decade of the new century, and then its sudden retreat, can be explained considering different factors.

First of all, note that in Italy households' investment decisions are mainly bank driven, meaning that—thanks to their marketing abilities—banks have historically been able to induce retail investors to buy what the banks want. Only recently, thanks to the introduction of MiFID I in 2007,[16] a major emphasis (and control) has been put on the adequacy of financial products with respect to the risk profile of investors.[17]

Consequently, when banks need to increase their long-term funding—as it happened during the credit boom—they tend to push depositors to subscribe bonds. On the other, when there is not a particular need to raise long-term funding, banks tend to sell other kinds of instruments to depositors. It is indeed well known that bank bonds issuance and the placement of mutual funds and insurance products (which are not direct funding, but allow banks to raise non-interest revenues) are inversely correlated; this was the case in the last few years, and the phenomenon is well represented in Fig. 2.6.

Figure 2.6 shows a decrease of 36, 74 and 71 billions, in 2013, 2014 and 2015, respectively, in banks' bonds held by households. In the same years, holdings of Italian government bonds diminished of 36, 31 and 32 billions of Euro, respectively. In contrast, we had a jump of 32, 56 and 43 billions of Euro in investment funds, and a 23, 53 and 49 billions of Euro increase in pension funds and life products.

Second, Italian households' investment decisions are strongly correlated to expected (or better granted) rates of return. Indeed, it is not inappropriate to say that Italian savers have not paid great attention to efficient portfolio construction and diversification, at least until recently. Throughout the 1990s, a strong home bias characterized their portfolios, tilted to Italian government securities: in fact, Italian government bonds, mistakenly considered risk free in domestic savers' mind, granted an interesting return. With the beginning of the Euro era, and with the blast of the New Economy bubble (which Italian savers rode by investing in high-tech mutual funds), the search for safe

[16]MiFID I stands for 'Markets in Financial Instruments Directive 2004', a European Union law that provides harmonized regulation for investment services across member states of the European Economic Area.

[17]Actually, also before MiFID I Italian legislation required banks to comply with adequacy rules, and to act in the best interest of clients. So, we are not saying here that the behaviour of banks was fraudulent (even if sometimes it was indeed), but surely (using a famous expression by Richard Thaler) credit institutions were able to "gently nudge" investors to subscribe financial instruments which were in the best interest of banks too.

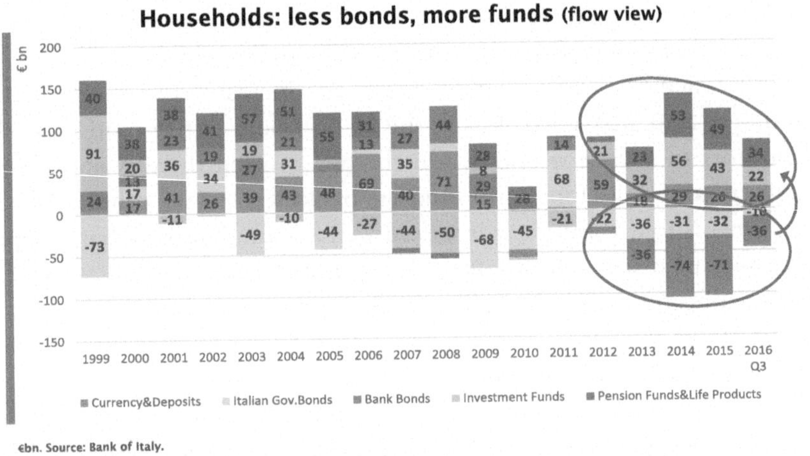

Fig. 2.6 Changing composition of households' wealth (flow view). *Source* Assogestioni (2017), *The Italian Asset Management market key figures*

(but in any case substantial)[18] returns facilitated the choice for banks' bonds at the beginning of the new century. Figure 2.6 shows how in 1999–2002 incremental flows of investments in banks' bonds were substantial (+24, +13, +23, +19 billions of Euro, respectively). Overall, banks were considered safe at that time (*bail-in* was indeed an unborn expression). In addition, to increase the appeal of their bonds, banks introduced interesting innovations in their structures: as we will see in Chap. 3, index-linked bonds, currency-linked bonds, structured bonds *et similia* became common in Italian savers' portfolios. Later, the post-crisis period, marked by a sharp decrease in interest rates, contributed (*inter alia*) to push household investments away from government securities and banks' bonds.

Another interesting aspect regarding households' holdings of banks' bonds is related to the issuer category. Once again, we follow the analysis of Coletta and Santioni (2016), which underscores a big difference between the five largest banking groups and small intermediaries. As regards the formers, the percentage of bonds held by families on total bonds outstanding reached in 2015 a level of about 40%. This is surely

[18]Italian savers yet seem to not have correctly understood the strong relationship between risk and return.

a significant level. Nevertheless, it implies that major banking groups are also, and mainly, able to place their debt securities to wholesale investors. A totally different situation resulted instead for small banks, which placed about 90% of their bonds to households (this was surely the case of small cooperative banks). For the system as a whole, the average share of bonds held in households' portfolios was between 40 and 50% of the total amount outstanding.

The aforementioned figures are fundamental to better interpret the Italian banks' bond market. Contrary to common belief—according to which bond buyers should be able to evaluate (at least in a partial efficient manner) risk and return profiles of the debt instruments and the related issuing entities—it is clear that if the majority of banks' bonds is placed to 'uneducated' retail investors, then the efficiency of the market is sharply reduced. Consequently, some theoretical reasoning—about the banks' funding strategies and the determinants of bonds issuance that we provided in Chap. 1—could not properly work in the Italian banks' bond market.

This means, as we will show in Chap. 4, that the spread between banks' bonds and government bonds yields, having the same maturity, could also be negative (as it happened in Italy some years ago), despite the higher credit and liquidity risk characterizing banks.[19] Additionally, the relationship between credit ratings and bond issuance is not probably so incisive in the domestic market.

Finally, a few words about the characteristics of banks' bonds held by Italian households need to be spent. At the end of 2015, about 63% of them was classified as 'plain vanilla'. 'Structured products', in which a derivative component is present (so that the return of the bond is linked to some underlying asset, such as a stock exchange, currency or commodity index), accounted for about 21%. 'Subordinated bonds', in which the reimbursement right in case of default is postponed after the reimbursement of other creditors (but not shareholders), had a weight of 14%—significantly higher than the 8% level registered in

---

[19]A great number of bonds issued by small and medium banks are not listed in a regulated market, or traded by a specialized market maker. In this case, the issuing bank itself usually acts as a dealer, although without granting continuous quotations or acceptable bid-ask spreads.

2009. Once again, there is a certain heterogeneity regarding the type of bank: for example, structured bonds were largely used by the five largest banking groups, while small banks almost issued entirely plain vanilla instruments.[20]

As regards the residual maturity, in 2015 it was up to 2 years for 46.1% of the bonds held by families; only 19.6% had a residual maturity longer than 5 years. Finally, the largest amount of bonds belongs to the fixed-interest category.[21]

2.5 Conclusions

The analysis of the funding strategies adopted by the Italian banks over the last ten years has confirmed the trends observed for the banks operating in the major European countries. Indeed, since late 2012 deposits have been steadily growing, the weight of bonds, compared to the liabilities, has sharply declined.

The evidence highlights as well that, after a peak of 11% reached in 2011, at the end of 2016 the share of households' wealth invested in banks' bonds was around 3.3% only. The data have also highlighted an important peculiarity of the Italian bank bonds market. Namely, until 2007 banks were used to place the majority of their bonds to households. After a steady decline throughout the years, at the end of 2016 only 25% of bank bonds appeared to be in retail investors' portfolios.

Overall, this underscores the key role played by the banks in guiding households' investments decisions. Our analysis has also shed some light on the opacity that has so far characterized the behaviour held by banks when placing their bonds to retail customers. In this regard, the transparency requirements introduced via MiFID II should lean towards an increasing reduction of banks' opportunistic conducts.

---

[20]See, in this regard, Coletta and Santioni (2016).

[21]This category includes plain vanilla fixed coupon bonds, zero coupon and stepped bonds.

References

Accornero, M., Finaldi Russo, P., Guazzarotti, G., Nigro, V., 2015. First-time corporate bond issuers in Italy. Bank of Italy Occasional Papers No. 269.

Assogestioni, 2017. The Italian Asset Management market key figures, March. Available at: http://www.assogestioni.it/index.cfm/3,870,11786/2017-03-28-the-italian-am-mkt-key-facts-feb-2017-update.pdf.

Bank of Italy, 2016. Financial Stability Report No. 1, Rome.

Bank of Italy, 2017a. Statistical Bulletin, Quarter 2. Available at: https://www.bancaditalia.it/pubblicazioni/bollettino-statistico/2017-bolstat/en_bolstat_2_2017.pdf?language_id=1.

Bank of Italy, 2017b. Annual Report for 2016. Available at: https://www.bancaditalia.it/pubblicazioni/relazione-annuale/2016/en_rel_2016.pdf?language_id=1.

Coletta, M., Santioni, R., 2016. Le obbligazioni bancarie nel portafoglio delle famiglie italiane. Questioni di Economia e Finanza (Occasional Papers) No. 359, Banca d'Italia.

ECB, 2016. The euro area bank lending survey. Available at: https://www.ecb.europa.eu/stats/money/surveys/lend/html/index.en.html.

Grasso, R., Linciano, N., Pierantoni, L., Siciliano, G., 2010. Bonds issued by Italian banks. Risk and return characteristics. Consob Working Paper No. 67.

Jobst, A., Weber, A., 2016. Profitability and Balance Sheet Repair of Italian Banks. IMF WP/16/175.

3

The Different Types of Bonds Issued by Italian Banks: An Overview

Abstract In this Chapter we provide a description regarding the characteristics of the bonds issued by Italian banks, as well as the rules governing the issuance of debt instruments. By employing data from a comprehensive database including 9,160 outstanding bonds, we show that banks, in Italy, typically issue plain vanilla bonds. Moreover, provided that the majority of bonds are unlisted, we infer that banks in Italy have been historically used to place their debt securities to retail customers directly at their branches. Finally, using real examples of debt securities currently held by retail investors, we illustrate some innovative structures of bank bonds. The complexity behind these structures suggests that retail investors are probably unaware of the implicit risks of the bonds, because they normally tend to buy (upon trust) what the bank proposes.

Keywords Bank bonds · Bond characteristics · Subordinated bonds

F. Crespi and D. V. Mascia, *Bank Funding Strategies*, Palgrave Macmillan Studies in Banking and Financial Institutions, https://doi.org/10.1007/978-3-319-69413-9_3

3.1 Introduction

As highlighted in Chap. 2, the Italian bank bonds market has long been characterized by a strict link between households' investment decisions and the issuing choices of banks. On the one hand, banks bonds were one of the most important financial assets held by Italian households at least until 2012; on the other hand, bonds were among the main sources of external funding for Italian banks until a few years ago, and a great majority of these bonds were placed (especially by small banks) directly to retail depositors.

Another important aspect of the market, as we will see below, is that most of the bonds issued—are not only by small and medium banks (mostly operating as cooperatives) but also by the largest intermediaries—are not listed in any regulated market (stock exchange or multilateral trading facility). That contributes to a significant opacity of prices and issuing costs, which consequently leads to strong biases in the risk-return profile. As pointed out by Grasso et al. (2010), due to the modest size of the issuances and the absence of a secondary market,[1] the liquidity risk of many bonds was (and yet is) is very high. Notwithstanding, the returns offered by the bonds sold to retail investors used to be weakly related to credit and liquidity risks and, on average, lower than those of Italian government bonds with similar maturity.[2] In addition, returns offered to retail investors are (*ceteris paribus*) lower than that demanded by institutional investors.

Finally, it is worthy of note that, during the first years of the current century, Italian banks largely used a sort of 'legislative freedom' to introduce in the market innovative and complex bonds structures, such as index and equity linked bonds, inflation linked instruments, credit linked notes. Moreover, these bonds were often wrapped inside insurance products, thus to exploit a still laxer legislation. It is easy to infer

---

[1]For bonds not listed in a stock exchange or in similar trading venue (for example a multilateral trading facility), the secondary market is mainly represented by the quotes expressed by the issuing banks which act as dealers or, in the best case, as systematic internalizers.

[2]With regards to this aspect, see also the analysis made in Chap. 4 for the period following the introduction of the BRRD.

that the implicit risks of these instruments were not understandable by the vast majority of retail investors. Starting from 2005, and even more from 2009, the introduction of stricter adequacy rules by the financial Authority[3] has forced banks to opt for simpler structures.

The aim of this chapter is then to analyse the characteristics of bonds issued by Italian banks: to do that, we briefly illustrate the rules governing the issuance of debt instruments by banks. By employing a sample of 9,160 bonds issued by 408 banks in Italy, we then show which types of bonds are currently available in the market. Finally, we explain some innovative structures of the bank bonds by utilizing real examples of debt securities currently held by retail investors.

3.2 Rules and Legislation Governing Banks' Bonds Issuance: A Short Summary

The issuance of bonds, by banks, is firstly regulated by art. 12 of the '*Testo Unico Bancario*', the main law governing the Italian banking sector since 1993.[4] This article indicates that banks, regardless of their legal form (limited companies or cooperatives), can issues bonds, also convertibles, in registered form or bearer form. The issuance of non-convertible bonds is decided by the management body (i.e., the Board of Directors).

Interestingly, some articles of the civil code are not applied to banks' bonds issuances: in particular, limits regarding the amount of bonds issuable, normally applied to non-financial corporations, are excluded for banks. The issuance of non-convertible bonds, as well as the issuance

[3]In Italy, the main financial authorities are the Bank of Italy and Consob. While the first is mainly responsible for the capital adequacy of banks, the rules regarding the adequacy of financial instruments and investment services proposed to retail investors are set by Consob (the Italian companies and stock exchange Commission) in accordance to the European Legislation (i.e., MiFID I and II frameworks) and ESMA recommendations.

[4]This law has been frequently amended, over the years, to incorporate EU legislation in Italy.

of bonds convertible in securities of other companies (exchangeable bonds)[5] is governed by the Bank of Italy.

Other rules governing the issuance of banks bonds are included in another fundamental law enacted in 1998,[6] the '*Testo Unico della Finanza*' (or Draghi's law, from the name of its author). This law, *inter alia*, regulates the functioning of the financial markets, the provision of investment and asset management services, and the placement of financial instruments to retail investors.

Art. 94 of this law (in accordance with EU legislation) regulates the issuance of financial instruments to the general public, by requiring anyone who wants to implement a public offer to publish in advance a prospectus. In particular, when the public offer regards financial instruments for which Italy is Home Member State, the prospectus has to be sent in advance to Consob, and it cannot be published before approval by the same Authority.

It is well known (from art. 5 of the Directive 2003/71/EC), that the prospectus must contain all information that (according to the particular nature of the issuer and of the securities offered to the public or admitted to trading on a regulated market) is necessary to enable investors to make an informed assessment of the assets and liabilities, financial position, profit and losses, outlook of the issuer, and of any guarantor, and of the rights attached to such securities. This information shall be presented in an easy and understandable way. The same statement is expressed in art. 94 of the '*Testo Unico della Finanza*'.

In short, the prospectus should give retail investors clear and comprehensible information to understand the risk/return profile of the financial instruments offered. But, until 2005, banks were exempted

[5]For example, a bank can issue a bond that is convertible in shares of a corporation not included in the banking group. In this case, either the bank has the shares of the external corporation in its investment portfolio (and wants to divest its shareholding), or the bond contains some kind of derivatives that grants the possibility to exchange it with shares.

[6]Here again, the law was amended many times to introduce European legislation in Italy; notably, the transposition of MiFID I and MiFID II frameworks, and the implementation of the Directive 2003/71/EC regarding the prospectus to be published when securities are offered to the public or admitted to trading.

from the prospectus regulation, and could actually place bonds to their depositors providing just limited information.

In 2005, the law No. 262 eliminated this distortion by requiring banks the editing of a prospectus for the issuance of bonds. A limited exemption remained only for non-equity securities issued in a continuous or repeated manner by credit institutions provided that:

- these securities are not subordinated, convertible or exchangeable;
- these securities do not give the right to subscribe or to acquire other types of securities and that they are not linked to a derivative instrument;
- the total amount of the offer, over a period of 12 months, is less than 75,000,000 Euro.

In this case, just a simplified prospectus is required.[7] Anyway, it is important to point out that banks normally use a specific procedure to issue their bonds, which is the so-called 'base prospectus'.[8]

The base prospectus contains all relevant information concerning the issuer and the securities offered to the public: this means that the base prospectus can be used for more than a single bond issuance, and this becomes very useful for banks that frequently issue bonds over time. Normally, banks produce a base prospectus valid for 12 months that can contain the description of the characteristics of something like five to ten different types of bonds. Then, just before the issuance of a specific bond actually takes place, the final terms and conditions are published and sent to the Consob.[9]

[7]Note that this provision is stricter than that provided in the EU Legislation. Indeed, Directive 2003/71/EC totally exempts from the editing of a prospectus in case of such kinds of issuances. An important aspect of this rule (the simplified prospectus) is that it is applied only to "simple bonds". These are defined by Consob as: bonds denominated in Euro issued by European banks not containing subordination clauses; bonds for which the reimbursement is granted at maturity and are not linked to derivatives; bonds for which coupons are fixed or linked to simple and known external interest rate such as Euribor. Moreover, the level of liquidity of the bonds should be sufficient to grant a prompt divestment.

[8]See art. 5 of Directive 2003/71/EC and art. 6 of Consob Regulation No. 11971.

[9]The final terms contain, for instance, information about the amount issued and the amount effectively subscribed.

Besides the rules regarding the publishing and contents of the prospectus, two other documents enacted by Consob have influenced the issuing of banks' bonds. In March 2009, Consob (see Consob 2009) issued Communication No. 9019104 regarding 'The duty of intermediaries to behave correctly and transparently when they distribute illiquid products'.[10] In this document the Authority, considering the large dissemination of illiquid products in the Italian market (such as bank bonds, insurance products containing financial instruments, OTC derivatives, etc.), and that retail investors normally consider these instruments as low risky ones,[11] introduced a set of recommendations for distributors. First of all, Consob reiterated to banks the necessity to evaluate the compatibility of products offered to the profile and needs of the customers served. Then, the Communication urged banks to comply with disclosure rules in order to grant more transparency to clients. In particular, it was required to illustrate to retail investors the unbundling of the products, especially in the case of structured bonds including a derivative component. This meant for banks to express separately the fair value of the bond component, the fair value of the derivative component, and the implicit distribution costs.

Just to give an example, let's consider an inflation linked bond issued by Banca Carige, ISIN IT 004626195, 2010–2020. The unbundling of the product is the following:[12]

[10]The communication represents a level 3 document in the MiFID framework, that is interpretative guidelines that support the practical application of the European directive. Illiquid products are defined as those that determine (for investors) limitations in case of disinvestment, so that the disinvestment cannot be made in a reasonable time, or the price of disinvestment does not reflect a reasonable fair value achievable in a liquid market. Many banks' bonds, especially structured ones, were indeed illiquid at that time.

[11]The Authority also pointed out a rather widespread commercial bias in the distribution of these kinds of instruments. Indeed they were very profitable for the banks' sale networks (upfront fees could reach 5–8% levels) and, consequently, were often proposed not properly considering the adequacy rules introduced by MiFID I.

[12]The bond is a structured one composed by a zero coupon and a floor option on the European inflation. The unbundling of the bond is reported in the final terms of the issuance.

Value of the derivative component	24.25
Value of the bond component (zero coupon)	74.75
Production costs	0.50
Issuing costs	0.50
Issuing price	100.00

In this case, if the investor wanted to disinvest immediately (that is, the day after the issuing date) the bond, it could probably receive at least 74.75 (the zero coupon value) and then a part of the value of the derivative component (that in this type of bonds is normally an OTC derivative), but surely not the price paid of 100.

That is why the Communication urged banks to clarify to investors the value, in case of disinvestment, in the second just after the transaction. Moreover, the Communication forced intermediaries to include in the final terms of the issuance a comparison between the return of a simple instrument, mainly a government bond, having the same maturity and the expected returns of the bond in three possible scenarios (negative, intermediate, positive). This last provision had a strong impact, because it revealed to investors that, in many cases, the expected return of the bond, even in the best scenario, was lower than the fixed return of a government bond. Here again, as example, we report the comparison for the above mentioned inflation linked bond issued by Banca Carige in 2010.

	Government bond (BTP 4% 1 September 2020)	Banca Carige bond
Maturity	1 September 2020	10 August 2020
Price	99.971	100
		Scenarios: Negative—Intermediate—Positive
Gross return (%)	4.04	2.22—2.27—2.92
Net return[a] (%)	3.53	1.94—1.98—2.56

[a]At the issuing date (2010) the tax rate for government bond and banks' bond was the same, 12.50%. Note that today the tax rate for bank bonds is 26%

Finally, the Communication No. 9019104 explained that when a structured bond including a derivative component is proposed to a retail investor, the intermediary must check if that investor has the adequate level of competence and experience to understand the risk of the derivative component, and not just the risk of the bond globally considered (that is, not unbundled). It is easy to understand that, usually, the majority of retail investors are able to understand the risk of a plain vanilla bond, but lack of an adequate level of competence to assess the risk of a derivative component. Consequently, this provision strongly limited the possibility to place structured bonds to retail customers, even if it did not represent a total ban.

In 2014, another Communication by Consob (i.e., No. 0097996) introduced additional limitations. This Communication followed the ESMA Opinion 2014/146 regarding 'MiFID practices for firms selling complex products'[13] and ESMA Opinion 2014/332 regarding 'Structured Retail Products. Good practices for product governance arrangements' (see ESMA 2014a, b).

In the first document, the European Authority explained how—due to (i) low returns from more traditional forms of investments or ordinary deposits, and (ii) volatility in the markets—investment firms had responded to the demand for higher yields by making alternative and more sophisticated investment strategies available to retail clients, often through complex investment products (including structured products). These complex products allowed retail investors access to asset classes, market segments and investment strategies that, previously, were only available to professional clients.

From an investor protection perspective, this trend poses certain risks for retail investors: due to the complexity of these products, investors may not be able to understand their risks, costs and expected returns and/or the drivers of risks and returns. This hampers their ability to make informed investment decisions, and increases the likelihood of consumer detriment (for example, unexpected losses).[14]

---

[13]Complex products/financial instruments are those that do not meet the criteria of "non-complex" as set out in Article 19 (6) of MiFID and Article 38 of the MiFID Implementing Directive.

[14]Note that Consob recognized that complexity does not always mean risk: actually, you can have complex products that are not risky or, inversely, simple products that are very risky. Notwithstanding, Consob considered fundamental that an investor could understand the structure of a product, in order to avoid unaware purchases.

ESMA opinion gives a list of examples of complex products:

1. they are derivatives, or embed a derivative; and/or
2. they are made up of one or more underlying financial instrument(s) that are difficult to value, or are combined in such a way so as to make it difficult to assess the risks involved and the likely performance scenarios; and/or
3. they use more opaque indices that are, for example, set up by the product manufacturer, rather than using standard market indices; and/or
4. have a fixed investment term of a number of years with barriers to exit (that are not clearly explained)—whether that is due to the lack of a secondary market, or significant penalties or losses on early exit; and/or
5. have returns/pay-off structures involving multiple variables or complex mathematical formulas; and/or
6. include capital protection that may be conditional or partial, or that can be withdrawn on the occurrence of certain events.

The following specific products should be considered as examples of complex products: contracts for difference (CFDs); binary options; turbos; exchangeable bonds; callable bonds; puttable bonds; convertible bonds; perpetual bonds; subordinated bonds; warrants; certificates; derivatives relating to underlying securities, currencies, interest rates, yields, or commodities; credit linked notes; and asset-backed securities.

Overall, the vast majority of structured products can be considered as complex products, so that many bank bonds (that are not in a plain vanilla form) are to be included in this category. In addition, ESMA Opinion 2014/332 defines 'Structured Retail Products' (SRPs) as compound financial instruments that have the characteristic of combining a base instrument (such as a note, fund or deposit) with an embedded derivative that provides economic exposure to reference assets, indices or portfolios. In this form, they provide investors, at predetermined times, with pay-offs that are linked to the performance of reference assets, indices or other economic values. Here again, many bank bonds are indeed SRPs.

ESMA Opinion 2014/146 and ESMA Opinion 2014/332 indicate, *inter alia*, that:

- If it appears that a particular complex product will never meet the best interests of the clients, or there is a lack of sufficient information available to ascertain the main features and risks of a product, National Authorities should monitor that investment firms do not offer advice on that envisaged product, or sell it at all.
- Notwithstanding the factors that manufacturers employ when designing SRPs, it is good practice for manufacturers to ensure they meet the financial needs, investment objectives, knowledge and experience of the target market identified by the manufacturer.
- It is good practice for distributors of SRPs to appropriately identify and analyse the target market for each SRP they intend to distribute.
- When SRPs are not listed on a liquid secondary market, it is good practice for firms to offer exit opportunities to investors who may need to sell the SRP before its end term and disclose those opportunities appropriately to the investor. It is good practice for 'exit prices' of non-listed SRPs (i.e., the price at which the investor may sell its SRP before its final term) to be determined using objective and pre-defined methodologies of which investors should be informed in advance.

The general idea behind the above-mentioned provisions is that a complex or structured product should always be in line with the characteristics of a specific and stated target market, namely it should not be proposed or sold to anyone who is outside the target market. And both the manufacturer and the distributor of the product (when they are not the same entity)[15] have to evaluate which is the right target market for the structured bond.

[15]This was (and is) frequently the case that occurs when a small bank issued a structured bond. The small bank acts as distributor, while the structured bond is normally manufactured by a specialized intermediary (for example an investment bank).

In its Communication No. 0097996/2014, Consob was even clearer to urge banks not to propose or distribute to retail investors the following products:

- Financial products arising from securitization processes (Asset Backed Securities, ABS);
- Financial products including convertible clauses in which, under certain conditions or at the initiative of the issuer, the product can be transformed in shares or an hair-cut to nominal value is possible;
- Credit linked notes;
- Derivative instruments not listed in trading venues (when they are not proposed as hedging tools);
- Structured products not listed in trading venues in which the pay-off profile does not guarantee the total reimbursement of the capital invested by retail investors.

In case an intermediary, under its responsibility, wants to disregard the recommendation of the Authority (because the intermediary considers it adequate, for the clients' interests, to propose one of the above mentioned products, and sufficient information is available to value the risks of the product):

- a specific and motivated decision about the commercialisation of such product must be adopted by senior management;
- the intermediary must consider and clearly demarcate the characteristics of the target market (level of competence, age, risk profile etc.) and the arrangements for the selling of such product;
- the intermediary must in any case inform the client that such product is not considered suitable for retail investors by the Authority.

For other complex products not included in the list above (for example, perpetual bonds or structured bond listed in a trading venue)—for which there is no specific indication saying that they are not suitable for retail investors—the Communication (following ESMA Opinions) imposes in any case stricter rules. In particular, intermediaries should pay greater attention with regards to the investors' profiling, thus to better understand their experience and competence about financial instruments. In short, the Communication No. 0097996/2014 by Consob, and the ESMA Opinions, made it more complicated and risky (from a legal point of view) for banks to issue or distribute bonds in a different form from the plain vanilla one, even if they did not totally rule out this possibility.

3.3 The Main Features of Italian Bank Bonds: Evidence from a Comprehensive Database

In order to investigate the characteristics of bonds issued by Italian banks, we illustrate hereafter an analysis of a dataset composed by 9160 bonds. We carry out our analyses by utilizing data from 'eXact 4 Suite', a platform provided by Analysis, an Italian joint-stock company operating as information provider for institutional investors and financial advisors.[16]

For our purposes, we retrieved the bulk of information on all the Italian banks' bonds (i.e., listed and unlisted) available at the beginning of August 2017. It is not our aim, here, to investigate the specific characteristics of every single bond, neither to explore the determinants of bonds issuance through an econometric model (as in Van Rixtel 2015, for example), but just to have an 'aerial view' of the market.

Therefore, apart from the name of the issuing bank, we gathered qualitative information about the following aspects:

- the listing of the bond (listed or unlisted),
- the seniority (senior or subordinated),

[16]In particular, the platform is very popular among financial advisors in Italy, as it allows simulations, construction, and monitoring of ideal diversified portfolios that advisors may build and recommend to their customers. Moreover, one of the strengths of this platform is that it offers daily updates about a variety of newly issued instruments such as mutual funds, corporate and government debt instruments, bank bonds, stocks and currencies as well.

- the return profile (fixed income; fixed + floating; fixed + zero coupon; floating; zero coupon),[17]
- the nature of the bond (Convertibles, Covered Bond, Credit Linked Notes, Currency Linked, Equity Linked, Fund Linked, Index Linked, Inflation Linked, Interest Rate Linked, Perpetual Preferred Securities, Plain Vanilla, Redeemable Bond),
- the issuance and maturity dates.

The dataset include 9,160 bonds issued in Italy by 408 banks. Table A2 in the Appendix lists the banks according to the number (not the nominal value) of outstanding bonds (from the highest to the lowest). As one can observe from the last Column (i.e., Total)—where we compute the share of every single bank's issuances over the total—the top places are occupied by largest banking groups, such as Banco BPM (390 outstanding bonds, 4.26% of the sample), UBI Banca, Intesa Sanpaolo,[18] Banca Nazionale del Lavoro, and Unicredit (376, 314, 270 and 252 outstanding bonds, respectively). But also a small bank such as 'Cassa Risparmio Asti', operating in the Northwest of the Boot, appears among the frequent users of bonds.

Overall, the first five issuers account for 17.49% of the total sample observations. If we go further along the table, we note that just 15 banks out of 408 (that is less than 4% of the intermediaries) issued more than 30% of the total outstanding bonds, and 50% of the bonds have been issued by only 46 financial institutions (that is about 11% of the banks in the sample). The market seems to be rather concentrated, indeed. However, it is worth noting that also very small banks (mainly cooperatives), have a number of outstanding bonds that is often greater than 30: just as an example, 'BCC Cremasca e Mantovana'

[17]Fixed + floating refers to bonds in which the periodical coupon is fixed for the first years, and then it is linked to an external interest rate such as Euribor. Fixed + zero coupon refers to bonds in which the periodical coupon is fixed for the first years; then, at a certain point in time, if some external conditions occur (for example a reference rate is higher or lower than a prefixed level), the coupon could be zeroed, so that the bond becomes a zero coupon.

[18]Note that Banca IMI (7th place) is the investment bank of Intesa Sanpaolo banking group.

operates through 39 bank offices in just 6 counties,[19] and has 33 bonds outstanding.

Another relevant information that emerges from the final raw of Table A2 is that the majority of bonds are not listed in a regulated market. Indeed, unlisted securities are 6,971, which correspond to more than 75% of the sample observations. These numbers corroborate the view that, in Italy, banks mostly place their bonds to retail customers directly at their branches and, later on, the secondary market is represented only by the opaque bid-ask spread quotations proposed by the issuing bank itself.

If we look at the return characteristics, we observe that the majority of bonds (i.e., 6,197, corresponding to more than 67% of the sample) offer a fixed coupon. Floating rate bonds, instead, are 1,607, corresponding to about 17.5% of the total observations. Bonds offering both a fixed and a floating coupon are 949 (10% of the sample), whereas zero coupon bonds are only about 4% (i.e., 396 bonds in total). Additionally, Table A2 displays information about the bond seniority. Here we find that senior bonds cover the vast majority of the sample as they amount to 8517 units (i.e., almost 93% of the sample). Overall, it is appropriate to say that the changes in legislation occurred in the last years (see Sect. 3.2), have forced banks to mostly issue plain vanilla fixed rate bonds.

Another important information—although not shown in the table—concerns the maturities of bonds at the issuing date. Throughout the sample, the average maturity of the bonds is 6.48 years (standard deviation 4.79). Obviously, this is very rough information, provided that the sample is quite heterogeneous. Just to give an idea, the maturity ranges and the number of bonds in each range are the following:

- up to one year (just one observation),
- from one year to two years (63 bonds),
- from two years to three years (604 bonds),
- from three years to four years (1,281 observations),
- from four years to five years (1,331 bonds),

[19] The total number of counties in Italy is 110.

- from five years to seven years (2,978 bonds),
- from seven years to ten years (1,243 bonds),
- from ten years to fifteen years (991 observations),
- from fifteen years to twenty years (364 bonds),
- from twenty years to thirty years (246 cases),
- Finally 58 bonds with a maturity of over 30 years including two very exceptional cases of a 60-year and a 70-year maturity bond.

Overall, about 68% of the bonds have a maturity of up to 7 years, and about 82% have a maturity lower or equal to 10 years. This means that banks mostly use bonds as a medium-term source of funding, rather than a long-term one. As a comparison, mortgages granted to households to buy a house usually have a maturity longer than ten years. Moreover, we have noticed that a lot of banks have been used to issue unlisted bonds very frequently during the year (once a month in many cases), so that the bonds produce a continued and revolving funding—as if they are a sort of deposit instrument—that banks directly place to retail investor at their branches.

We now present some other relevant information about the bond characteristics with the help of a few tables. Specifically, if we look at Panel A of Table 3.1 we observe that more than 70% of the subordinated bonds (458 in absolute numbers) are unlisted. This might again lead us thinking that banks may have taken advantage of their bargaining power to place risky bonds to retail customers rather than to more 'conscious' institutional investors. And this is not unlikely, especially if we consider the significant number of cases—come to light soon after the resolution of four small Italian banks in 2015—of retail investors that put their savings into unlisted subordinated bonds.[20] Moving along Table 3.1, we further observe from Panel B that the majority of bonds (almost 84%) are 'plain vanilla', thus implying that banks mostly prefer to issue simple bonds (e.g., with no derivative components attached). However, we still have a significant presence of index linked, inflation linked, redeemable and covered bonds.

[20]This case will be specifically discussed in Chap. 4.

Table 3.1 Listing of bonds vs seniority and type

	Listed	Unlisted	Total
Panel A—Seniority			
Senior	2,004	6,513	8,517
Subordinated	185	458	643
Total	2,189	6,971	9,160
Panel B—Type of bond			
Convertibles	0	6	6
Covered bond	72	85	157
Credit linked notes	0	3	3
Currency linked	3	0	3
Equity linked	2	4	6
Fund linked	1	2	3
Index linked	40	15	55
Inflation linked	10	18	28
Interest rate linked	194	315	509
Perpetual preferred	12	17	29
Plain vanilla	1,787	5,895	7,682
Redeemable bond	68	611	679
Total	2,189	6,971	9,160

Covered bonds, in particular, are innovative instruments introduced in Italy by the Law 80/2005, which amended Law 130/99 (the law regarding the securitization process). Essentially, covered bonds are bonds guaranteed by assets (such as mortgages or debts owed by Public administration) which are segregated in a special purpose vehicle (SPV). Contrary to traditional securitization schemes, in which securities are issued directly by the SPV, in this case the covered bonds are issued by the bank itself, while the SPV put a guarantee on them. In simple terms, these bonds are implicitly guaranteed by the issuing bank; in case of failure of the issuing banks the segregated collateral is used to repay bondholders.

If we look at Table 3.2, we then note that the majority of 'plain vanillas' are senior bonds (93%), whereas only 7% of them are subordinated (488 out of 7682). Furthermore, moving to the remuneration, in Panel A of Table 3.3 we find that about 73% of 'plain vanilla' bonds offer a fixed return, whereas 15% provide a floating remuneration. Finally, from Panel B we observe that 68% of the subordinated bonds (i.e., 438 out of 643) offer a fixed coupon.

Table 3.2 Seniority vs type of bond

Type of bond	Senior	Subordinated	Total
Convertibles	3	3	6
Covered bond	157	0	157
Credit linked notes	3	0	3
Currency linked	3	0	3
Equity linked	6	0	6
Fund linked	3	0	3
Index linked	55	0	55
Inflation linked	28	0	28
Interest rate linked	482	27	509
Perpetual preferred	2	27	29
Plain vanilla	7,194	488	7,682
Redeemable bond	581	98	679
Total	8,517	643	9,160

Table 3.3 Return vs type of bond and seniority

	Fixed	Fixed + Floating	Fixed + Zero C.	Floating	Zero C.	Total
Panel A—Type of bond						
Convertibles	6	0	0	0	0	6
Covered bond	73	0	0	84	0	157
Credit linked notes	2	0	0	1	0	3
Currency linked	0	1	0	0	2	3
Equity linked	0	3	0	0	3	6
Fund linked	1	1	0	0	1	3
Index linked	1	28	3	10	13	55
Inflation linked	0	19	0	7	2	28
Interest rate linked	6	276	1	226	0	509
Perpetual preferred	10	17	0	2	0	29
Plain vanilla	5,582	586	7	1,162	345	7,682
Redeemable bond	516	18	0	115	30	679
Total	6,197	949	11	1,607	396	9,160
Panel B—Seniority						
Senior	5,759	881	11	1,473	393	8,517
Subordinated	438	68	0	134	3	643
Total	6,197	949	11	1,607	396	9,160

Overall, the analysis of the aggregated data shows that, nowadays, Italian banks prefer:

1. to issue (simple) plain vanilla bonds (fixed rate or linked to well known reference rate such as the Euribor);
2. not to list their bonds in a regulated market;
3. to issue bonds with an average medium-term maturity.

3.4 The Characteristics of Bonds: Some Examples

We conclude this Chapter by presenting some examples about the characteristics of bonds outstanding in the market. It is not our purpose to illustrate all the possible structures and indexation mechanisms usable for engineering a bond (that would require a separate publication);[21] rather, we aim to offer the reader with an idea about some 'strange' bonds ended up in retail investors' portfolios, issued by both small and large intermediaries.

As indicated above, most of the bonds issued by Italian banks are plain vanilla, that is fixed rate bonds paying a periodical coupon and not redeemable before maturity. Many other bonds included in our dataset are floating rate bonds paying a coupon calculated as Euribor plus a given spread, which can be considered plain vanilla as well.

Then we have some index linked bonds, some inflation linked bonds and some interest rate linked bonds, in which the coupon can vary considerably according to the rules expressed in the final terms of the offer and, finally, redeemable bonds. We focus our attention on these last kinds of instruments, and we use the information provided in the final terms and conditions documents to describe them.

Let us start with a bond issued by 'Banca del Piemonte', ISIN IT0005073009. The issuing date is 19 January 2015 and the maturity date is 19 January 2020. The nominal value of each bond is 1,000 Euro,

[21]For a comprehensive analysis see Pampurini (2010) and Grasso et al. (2010).

so that it can easily be subscribed by retail investors. The bond pays a semi-annual coupon linked to 'Euribor 6 months' but, reading the final terms of the offer, we discover that the first four coupons are actually fixed (1% gross); later on, starting from July 2017, the coupon becomes variable, and it is linked to 'Euribor 6 months'. This means that the investor who bought the bond in 2015, would have had the following idea: 'I receive a very low fixed coupon in the first two years, but then I hope that a greater Euribor will provide me with a larger coupon'. Now, regardless of the market conditions after 2015 (and the fact that interest rates went below zero because of extraordinary monetary policy measures), the critical point is that the final terms indicate that, when the coupon becomes variable, it is limited by a floor and a cap rate (respectively 0.60% and 1.70%). So, if Euribor actually increases, the investor receives in any case a limited coupon.

A similar scheme is presented in the 'Banca Monte dei Paschi di Siena S.p.A. 2011/2017 TassoMisto Cap&Floor BancoPosta Serie 4' bond (ISIN IT0004761356). Interestingly, this bond was issued in 2011 by Monte Paschi di Siena, but was actually distributed by BancoPosta, the bank of the government owned Postal and Courier Services Company. The coupon paid by the bond is annual: here again, in the first two years the bond pays a fixed coupon of 5.5% (gross). Later on, the coupon not only is linked to 'Euribor 6 months', but it becomes semi-annual. So starting from 2014 and until its maturity date (2017), the bond pays a coupon calculated as 'Euribor 6 months' plus a given spread (1.40%) with a floor (4.60%) and a cap (5.40%). Even if at first sight the interest rates paid could seem conspicuous, it is worth noting that the final terms report a comparison between the return of the bond in three different scenarios (negative, intermediate, positive) and the return of a government bond with similar maturity. This comparison shows how the government bond, in any case, granted at the issuing date a greater return. Another interesting aspect of this bond can be found in the unbundling scheme (see below). The issuing price is 100% of the nominal value—that is 1,000. The value of the bond component is 939.85 and the value of the derivative component is 30.88.

Issuing price	1,000.00
Value of the bond component	939.85
Value of the derivative component	30.88
Issuing costs	29.27
Expected value after issuing date	970.73

Considering 29.27 of issuing costs (which is the revenue of BancoPosta for the distribution service), the expected value just after the issuing date is 970.73. That is, if the investor wanted to sell the bond the day immediately after the issuing date (this bond was actually listed in a regulated market), he had probably lost about 2.93% of the nominal value. It is finally worth noting that the target market for this bond (as indicated in the final terms document) should be formed by the investors with a medium level of competence and experience in financial investments, and characterized by a high risk appetite. However, it is well known that the average BancoPosta depositor is quite old and used to invest only in simple government guaranteed instruments.

Another interesting example is represented by a ten-year bond issued in 2009 by Banca Carige (ISIN IT0004518426). It is an inflation linked bond, but the coupon is limited by a floor and a cap rate. The bond was issued on 20 August 2009, with nominal value of 1,000 Euro and issuing price of 100% (of the nominal value). The bond is unlisted. On 20 August 2010, the bond paid a fixed coupon of 4% (gross). The following annual coupons are linked to HICP, the Eurostat Eurozone Harmonized Index of Consumer Prices Ex-Tobacco Unrevised. The formula to calculate the coupon is: 1% + max (0%; European inflation rate), meaning that if the European inflation rate is below zero the coupon is just 1%. To calculate the European inflation rate the issuer uses the following formula:

$$\textit{European inflation rate} = \frac{HICP_t}{HICP_{t-1}} - 1$$

$HICP_t$ is the inflation index in the month of May of period t, while $HICP_{t-1}$ is the value of the same inflation index 12 months before. The change in the value of the index between t–1 and t represents the inflation rate to be used to calculate the next year coupon. Hereby we provide a table to clarify the mechanism.

Coupon	Payment date	*t*–1	*t*
2	20 August 2011	May 2009	May 2010
3	20 August 2012	May 2010	May 2011
4	20 August 2013	May 2011	May 2012
5	20 August 2014	May 2012	May 2013
6	20 August 2015	May 2013	May 2014
7	20 August 2016	May 2014	May 2015
8	20 August 2017	May 2015	May 2016
9	20 August 2018	May 2016	May 2017
10	20 August 2019	May 2017	May 2018

It is easy to infer that the inflation rate of the previous year determines the coupon of the next year. This means that if the inflation increases in one year, only in the following year the investor will receive a greater coupon. And again: the unbundling of the product reported in the final terms indicates that 18.85% of the issuing price is due to the derivative component. The comparison with a government bond with similar maturity shows that only in the positive scenario the bond could produce a slightly higher return. Put it another way, the investor implicitly buys an expensive derivative component just to have a limited probability to earn a greater return than the one offered by a plain vanilla government bond.

Finally, a bond (ISIN IT0004980485) issued by a primary bank, Banca IMI, which is the investment bank of Intesa Sanpaolo Banking group, one of the two largest players of the market (the other being Unicredit). Usually, the bonds issued by Banca IMI are listed in a regulated market. In recent years, Banca IMI used even a rather innovative issuing mechanism, placing its bonds directly in the secondary market. Notwithstanding, here we focus on an unlisted bond. Below we provide the characteristics of the bond.

Nominal value 1,000 Euro. Issuing price 100% (of the nominal value). Issuing date 31 January 2014. Fixed annual coupon paid (2.70%) at the following dates: 31 January 2015, 31 January 2016, 31 January 2019, 31 January 2020. It is easy to observe that in 2017 and

2018 no fixed coupon is paid. Indeed, the bond pays on 31 January 2017 and 31 January 2018 two 'digital' coupons (this is exactly how they are called) linked to a stock exchange index, namely 'EURO STOXX 50'. The amount of the digital coupons is 5% or 0% depending on the occurrence of a specified condition. In simple words, the performance of 'EURO STOXX 50', calculated at the dates of the digital coupon payments, must be higher than a prefixed level (the barrier) of 10%. The performance of 'EURO STOXX 50' is calculated as: the percentage difference between the value of the index on 23 January 2017 and on 31 January 2014 (for the first digital coupon); the percentage difference between the value of the index on 23 January 2018 and on 31 January 2014 (for the second digital coupon).

As mentioned above, the bond is issued by Banca IMI. However, the final terms show that it is distributed exclusively by Banca Popolare di Milano. In the end, the depositors of Banca Popolare di Milano are those who actually buy the bonds. Banca Popolare di Milano, as distributor, receives a commission of 2.80% of the nominal value.

The few examples reported above provide, in our opinion, a significant evidence of the complexity and opacity regarding the placement of some bank bonds to retail investors. As pointed out elsewhere, Italian banks not only copiously used bonds as a funding instrument—which could be in any case fair where the bonds ensure an adequate rate of return—but they also nudged their depositors to buy 'appealing' debt instruments which were mainly issued for the interest of the bank, especially when it acted as distributor and simply received a commission.

3.5 Conclusions

In this Chapter, we provided a description regarding the characteristics of the bonds issued by Italian banks, as well as the rules governing the issuance of debt instruments. Moreover, by employing data from a comprehensive database including 9,160 outstanding bonds, we have shown that banks, in Italy, typically issue plain vanilla (unlisted) bonds. Such evidence corroborates the findings of the previous Chapter that highlighted the key role of banks in guiding households' investments decisions. Indeed, provided that the majority of bonds are unlisted, we infer that banks in Italy have been historically used to place their debt securities to retail customers directly at their branches. Therefore, it is not incorrect to say that the Italian bank bonds market is not efficient. Additionally, much of the academic reasoning about the determinants of bonds issuance (e.g., market discipline, risk-return correlation, optimal capital structure and so on) appears inappropriate when applied to Italy.

Finally, using real examples of debt securities currently held by retail investors, we have illustrated some innovative structures of bank bonds. The complexity behind these structures suggests that retail investors are probably unaware of the implicit risks of the bonds, because they normally tend to buy (upon trust) what the bank proposes.

References

Consob, 2009. Il dovere dell'intermediario di comportarsi con correttezza e trasparenza in sede di distribuzione di prodotti finanziari illiquidi. Comunicazione No. 9019104, 2 Marzo.

Grasso, R., Linciano, N., Pierantoni, L., Siciliano, G., 2010. Bonds issued by Italian banks. Risk and return characteristics. Consob Working Paper No. 67.

ESMA, 2014a. MiFID practices for firms selling complex products.

ESMA, 2014b. Structured retail products—Good practices for product governance arrangements.

Pampurini, F., 2010. Le obbligazioni strutturarte. ISEDI, Novara.

Van Rixtel, A., Gonzalez, L.R., Yang, J., 2015. The determinants of long-term debt issuance by European banks: Evidence of two crises. BIS Working Papers No. 513.

4

The Bail-in Effect: How the Cost of Funding Through Bonds has Changed After the Introduction of the BRRD

Abstract By employing data from a unique hand-collected dataset, in this Chapter we show that, since the adoption of the BRRD in the European Union, Italian banks—probably motivated by the need to increase the appeal of their *bail-inable* debt instruments—have been forced to offer higher yields (compared to the yields offered by government securities with corresponding maturities) to bondholders, with the consequence of an increase in their cost of funding. Finally, we conclude this final Chapter by offering some very recent examples about the application of the BRDD rules in Italy—which have either led to liquidation, resolution, or precautionary recapitalization cases—and the related side effects generated to bank bondholders.

Keywords Bond yields · Cost of funding · BRRD · Bail-in tool Resolution · Liquidation

F. Crespi and D. V. Mascia, *Bank Funding Strategies*, Palgrave Macmillan Studies in Banking and Financial Institutions, https://doi.org/10.1007/978-3-319-69413-9_4

4.1 Introduction

It is widely acknowledged that the Global Financial Crisis—yet erupted ten years ago—led to important interventions by national governments aimed at bailing out failing banks. Just to give an idea of the phenomenon, during the years 2008–2012 European governments contributed to restore the financial sector—via capital injections and asset reliefs (excluding guarantees)—with about 600 billion Euros, namely 4.6% of 2012 European GDP (Benczur et al. 2016).

These numbers clearly highlight why such way of resolving banks' failures was not sustainable anymore. Specifically, the probability of a bail-out leads to moral hazard phenomena—i.e., the bankers are likely to take on more risk as they are aware that the cost of a possible failure will be borne by taxpayers (ECB 2016; Hüser et al. 2017). Furthermore, such a system leads to unfair competitions among banks. Indeed, a bank whose assets are backed by a state guarantee will be perceived safer by investors who will ask for lower risk premiums. This, in turn, means that systemically important institutions can raise money at cheaper rates than smaller banks (Ueda and Weder di Mauro 2013). This is particularly true in a bail-out regime.

To curb this practice, a new resolution framework was put in place via the Bank Recovery and Resolution Directive (BRRD) that introduced the bail-in tool (applicable since 1st January 2016). The idea behind this tool is that the cost of a bank failure is now shifted from taxpayers to the bank's shareholders and its creditors. More technically, through the bail-in tool, the Resolution Authority[1] has the power to write down and convert into equity the claims of a series of creditors (included unsecured bondholders) following a top down scheme, namely considering the seniority of the different instruments involved. However, this system properly works (i.e., the upfront implicit state guarantee available to all banks is credibly removed) when i) banks are resolvable with no need of state aid (i.e., when a bank can

[1] In Italy, the Resolution Authority is the Bank of Italy.

autonomously bear its losses via a bail-in driven recapitalization); ii) the resolution does not generate significant contagion risk (see, for instance, Hüser et al. 2017).

In light of the aforementioned substantial regulatory change, in this chapter we offer evidence, supported with real data, of the effect that the implementation of such rules has had on the cost of funding borne by Italian banks when they use bonds. More specifically, provided that the bail-in tool may also affect bank bondholders, we study the response of private investors on the pricing of new bond issuances. Furthermore, in the final part of this chapter, we offer a description of the most significant episodes, occurred until July 2017, regarding the application of the BRRD to some Italian banks.

The chapter is structured as follows. Section 4.2 offers a brief explanation of the principles governing the BRRD and the European Banking Union overall. Section 4.3 provides a focus on the well-known *bail-in* tool. Section 4.4 offers an empirical analysis about the effects that the implementation of the BRRD may have generated on the cost of funding through bonds borne by Italian banks. Section 4.5 presents some case studies on the application of the BRDD rules in Italy. Finally, Sect. 4.6 offers conclusions.

4.2 The BRRD

The Global Financial Crisis, erupted in August 2007, was a period characterized by financial instability for the global financial systems, mainly attributable to problems within large intercon nected banks. To restore stability and confidence in the markets, Governments utilized public sources to rescue failing banks thus avoiding their bankruptcy: the so-called *bail-out* was largely used. However, this was possible at the expenses of taxpayers, who actually bore the losses in lieu of the banks' shareholders.

Given the enormous costs generated by the crisis, and the fact that within a *bail-out* framework banks are typically inclined to take on more risk (moral hazard phenomenon), a call for a new regulation aimed at reducing the occurrence and the impact of new banking crises arose. Therefore, in 2011 the G20 Financial Stability Board proposed harmonized standards for the resolution of (systemic) banks (see World Bank Group 2016a). The European Union promptly followed the suggested guidelines and, in 2014, issued the so-called BRRD.[2] Basically, the BRRD offers a unique set of rules to be followed for the recovery and resolution of EU banks.[3]

Overall, the predominant goal of the BRRD is ensuring the possibility to quickly resolve banks, limiting the (negative) effects on financial markets and on the real economy as well as avoiding any burden on taxpayers—*de facto* implying the move from a *bail-out* to a *bail-in* regime. In this way, the BRRD is also able to put an end to the harmful link between banks and sovereigns that characterized the Euro area debt crisis (see, for instance, Mascia et al. 2017). Specifically, the intents explicitly set out in the BRRD (Article 31(2)) are: '*(a) to ensure the continuity of critical functions (of a bank in distress); (b) to avoid a significant adverse effect on the financial system, in particular by preventing contagion, including to market infrastructures, and by maintaining market discipline; (c) to protect public funds by minimising reliance on extraordinary public financial support; (d) to protect depositors covered by Directive 2014/49/EU and investors covered by Directive 97/9/EC; (e) to protect client funds and client assets*'.

Technically, the BRRD is based on the following elements:

- Recovery and resolution plans;
- Early interventions measures aimed at preventing the occurrence of new crises;
- Resolution tools introduced in order to ensure that shareholders and creditors are the ones actually bearing losses. The resolution tools are:

[2]The Directive is available at the following link: http://eur-lex.europa.eu/legal-content/EN/TXT/?uri=CELEX:32014L0059.

[3]Note that, the BRRD together with the 2013 Capital Requirements and Regulation Directive (CRD IV—i.e., Basel III) and the 2014 Deposit Guarantee Scheme Directive (DGSD) form the so-called "**Single Rulebook**", which is the name associated to the rules governing the EU financial sector.

- The ***bail-in***—allowing for losses absorption by shareholders and creditors;
- The **sale of business**—the resolution authority is allowed to sell, even partly, the failing bank activities to private buyers;
- The **bridge institution**—good assets are transferred to a new institution (the bridge bank);
- The **asset separation**—bad assets are moved to an asset management vehicle for wind down.

- Limited Government support—only possible as very last resort;
- Ex-ante resolution funds—funded through contributions from banks (each bank contributes to the fund according to its size);
- Cooperation between EU Member States and authorities in third countries during the various preparation, intervention and resolution stages.

Having said that, in the next Section we provide the main traits of the bail-in tool, which represents an important innovation in the EU bank resolution toolkit.

Box 1—The European Banking Union
The European Banking Union, which rests upon the abovementioned single rulebook, has been created with the aim of centralizing the supervisory and resolution powers within the Eurozone (EU Member States outside the Eurozone may also join), thus to ensure a harmonized compliance to the EU rules (see Arnaboldi 2014). Moreover, the motivation behind the design of such a Union was to ensure integration as well as restoring confidence in the Euro area after the Sovereign Debt crisis.

The Banking Union consists of the following three pillars:

- The **Single Supervisory Mechanism** (SSM), which refers to the system of prudential supervision, comprises the European Central Bank (ECB) and the National Competent Authorities (NCAs). As of April 2017, the ECB directly supervises 124 'significant' banks (ECB 2017), which represent about 80% of the Euro area bank assets. Smaller banks, instead, are supervised by NCAs (and, indirectly, by the ECB). However, starting from 2018, also small and medium banks will be partially subject to the ECB control.
- The **Single Resolution Mechanism** (SRM), created to ensure an orderly resolution of failing banks with minimal impact on the real economy

and, possibly, no costs to taxpayers. The SRM consists of i) the ***Single Resolution Board*** (SRB) and ii) the ***Single Resolution Fund*** (SRF)—the SRF, gradually funded by the banking industry, is owned and administrated by the SRB. Both the SRB and the SRF became fully operational in January 2016. Notably, the SRB is the resolution authority for banks considered 'significant' and other cross-border groups. As of December 2016, the banks under the remit of the SRB were 141, including 126 groups and other 15 cross-border groups (SRB 2017). National Resolution Authorities (NRAs), instead, are responsible for the resolution decisions regarding banks outside the remit of the SRB (i.e., small and non-cross-border banks). For the purpose of safeguarding financial stability, the SRB does not solely intervene in case a resolution occurs; rather, it proactively focuses on resolution planning and preparation in order to minimize possible negative effects of bank failure on the economy.

- The **European Deposit Insurance Scheme** (EDIS), whose competencies and powers have not been transferred to the European level yet. Indeed, the European Deposit Insurance is based on harmonized rules applied to all EU Member States, thus to ensure same purpose and level of deposit insurance (currently, deposits are ensured up to Euro 100,000 per person per bank). Negotiations are still undergoing at the European Commission and Council as for the creation of the EDIS, which would eventually complete the European Banking Union.

4.3 The Bail-in Tool

As previously stated, the scope of the new regulation is to avoid future *bail-outs*. Hence, for a resolution mechanism to be credible, the resolution funding arrangements need to be perceived as the very last resort instruments. Indeed, the Resolution Authority is first allowed to distribute losses to shareholders and debt-holders of the problematic bank (i.e., *bail-in*), according to a predefined creditor hierarchy. This implies that shareholders' interests are cancelled, or diluted, and creditors' claims are written down or converted into equity in order to recapitalize the bank: this procedure represents a remarkable change with the past.

It is also worthy of note that the BRRD provides that some liabilities are specifically excluded from the scope of the bail-in (e.g., covered bonds; deposits up to the amount covered by the deposit guarantee scheme; liabilities to tax and social security authorities; liabilities for contributions to deposit guarantee schemes; employees' remunerations; liabilities to other banks with an original maturity of less than seven days; liabilities with a remaining maturity of less than seven days, owed to payment or securities settlement systems; liabilities to commercial or trade creditors related to the provision of critical goods and services). In addition, the BRRD also allows the resolution authority to decide whether excluding some liabilities from the *bail in*—essentially when widespread contagion threatening the financial stability needs to be seriously averted (this mainly concerns deposits held by individuals and small and medium sized enterprises (SMEs)).[4]

When losses are not fully absorbed by shareholders and creditors, sources from the resolution fund can be utilized to cover the remaining unabsorbed losses, thus restoring to zero the net asset value of the bank, and/or to buy shares or other equity instruments to recapitalize the institution, thus restoring its Common Equity Tier 1 (CET1) ratio. However—and this is a fundamental feature of the BRRD—the use of Government support (when it does not interfere with the EU State Aid rules) and of the resolution fund are conditional on earlier 8% *bail-in*—where the 8% threshold is calculated against total liabilities including own funds.

After this brief description of the *bail-in* tool, we move to the following Section where we try to give a picture—supported with real data—regarding the effects that the new regulation may have generated on the banks' cost of funding.

[4]Note that when certain liabilities are excluded from the *bail-in*, the resolution authority may increase the write-down of other *bail-inable* liabilities. However, this is only possible if the losses suffered by the *bailed-in* creditors do not exceed the losses they would have borne in case the financial institution was put under liquidation. This is the so-called "no creditors worse off than under liquidation" (NCWOL) principle that resolution authorities need to keep in mind when applying resolution tools.

4.4 The Effect of *Bail-in* on the Cost of Funding Through Bonds of Italian Banks: An Empirical Analysis

When the news of a bank entering into troubles is spread by the media, depositors—also due to a lack of financial literacy—typically behave irrationally carrying out what is called a *bank run*. Indeed, outflows of deposits from problematic institutions to safer (at least according to depositors' perceptions) banks occur, even when a substantial deposit insurance scheme is in place in a given country.

This occurrence is not new in the literature. Such phenomena have been recorded in a variety of circumstances, even under the previous—more favourable, at least for depositors—*bail-out* regime (see, for instance, Peia and Vranceanu 2017).[5] This is not inconsequential, provided that under the *bail-in* framework retail investors (owning, for instance, unsecured bank bonds) and depositors face a greater probability of incurring possible losses. Therefore, the threat of deposit outflows may be even greater than in the past. In a recent paper, Boccuzzi and De Lisa (2017) study the effect of the early application, in 2015, of the BRRD to four Italian failing banks. They find that, starting from the Special Administration procedure (decided by the Italian Resolution Authority, namely Bank of Italy), the resolved banks faced a remarkable loss of funding—basically due to a flight of depositors.

Therefore, it is interesting to further study whether, following the introduction of the BRRD, even the bank bonds market has in a manner reacted to such a change in the regulation. Notably, because bonds are included in the hierarchy of the *bail-inable* instruments, we expect that retail investors properly price the increased riskiness by demanding higher risk premium on bank bonds.

[5]Just to offer an example, think of the Latvian bank run occurred at the Swedish-owned Swedbank, in December 2011, due to uncontrolled depositors' panic. See, in this regard, 'Panic fuels Latvian run on bank', BBC, December 12, 2011, available at: http://www.bbc.co.uk/news/business-16142000.

Table 4.1 List of banks and related positions in the country ranking

Country rank by assets	Bank Name
1	UniCredit SpA
2	Intesa Sanpaolo
5	Banca Monte dei Paschi di Siena SpA
7	Unione di Banche Italiane Scpa
8	Banca Nazionale del Lavoro SpA
9	Mediobanca SpA
10	BPER Banca S.P.A.
12	Cassa di Risparmio di Parma e Piacenza SpA
19	Banca Popolare di Sondrio Societa Cooperativa per Azioni
20	Veneto Banca scpa
21	Banca Carige SpA
24	Banca Piccolo Credito Valtellinese
39	Cassa di risparmio di Asti SpA
40	Banco di Desio e della Brianza SpA
42	Unipol Banca Spa
50	Banca Popolare dell'Alto Adige Societa Cooperativa Per Azioni
66	Banca Agricola Popolare di Ragusa SCARL
101	Banca di Credito Cooperativo di Carate Brianza
109	Banca Passadore & C. SpA
N.A.	Banca Popolare di Milano SCaRL
N.A.	Banco Popolare

Hence, our intent in this Section is to provide evidence of a possible effect that the new *bail-in* regime has generated on the cost of funding borne by Italian banks, as measured by the interest rate offered on bank bonds.

To do so, we rely on a unique hand-collected dataset containing information gathered from the documents reporting the final terms of 1160 bank bond issuances made by 21 banks, chartered in Italy, during the period January 2013–December 2016. Table 4.1 provides the list of the issuing institutions, along with their positions in the country ranking (compiled according to the bank size), which highlights the heterogeneity of our sample—given the inclusion of small, medium and large banks.

More than 70% of the collected data concerns unlisted bonds. This is an important feature that contributes to the originality of our database. Indeed, most of the studies usually rely on data from standardized sources, such as Datastream or Dealogic, which mainly contain information on listed securities. Additionally, such peculiarity represents a further strength for our analysis, considering that, after 2012, small and medium banks have sold to retail customers about 80% of their bonds—which is a significantly higher figure than the one recorded by the five largest banking groups (Coletta and Santioni 2016). Put it differently, omitting unlisted bonds might produce an incomplete and biased representation of the phenomenon under investigation.

Because we are interested in analysing the impact that the adoption of the *bail-in* regime might have exerted on the banks' funding costs linked to the issuance of their own bonds, following Sironi (2003) we only rely on the yield to maturity at launch offered in the primary market. This implies that we are not interested on the secondary market pricing of the bank bonds, provided that it does not affect the cost that the bank bears on already placed bonds (Zaghini 2014).[6]

In addition, the vast majority of the observations in our sample (roughly 83%) refers to fixed interest rate bonds.[7] This is pivotal for our analysis as it allows us to obtain proper evidence of the *spread* between the bank bond yields and the yield offered by a Government bond with corresponding maturity.

The reason behind the choice of including only 21 banks comes from the need of being in a position to make a fair comparison between the issuances before and after the introduction of the *bail-in* regime. For this reason, we undertook a backward approach. Namely, we started collecting data from banks that—to the best of our knowledge—made a significant number of issuances in 2016 (that is the year in which the BRRD with its *bail-in* tool became fully operational), thus excluding those financial institutions that did not place a reasonable number of

[6]Note that, as suggested by Sironi (2003), we also avoid considering the secondary market because of the poor liquidity characterizing the majority of the (unlisted) bonds in our investigation.

[7]More precisely, almost 72% are fixed rate, and about 11% are step-up bonds; the remaining are floating.

bonds after the new regulatory regime. Then, for those selected banks, we backward collected data on previous issuances made throughout the years 2013–2015. In this way, we are able to carry out reasonable comparisons between pre and post adoption periods.

Our data show that more than 200 bond issuances, per year, took place in the first three years of the sample period, with a peak registered in 2014 when they amounted to 435. In contrast, in 2016 only 172 bonds were issued, the majority of which during the first semester of the year. Such a contraction may be explained i) by the expansionary monetary policies implemented by the ECB during the last years (Bufacchi 2017), which considerably reduced the need of funding among retailers—provided that banks could fund themselves at lower costs via the Central Bank channel—as well as ii) by an overall reduction of the supplied loans.[8] Additionally, banks might have also decided to avoid issuing new debt financing for fear of a possible increase in the risk premium demanded by investors (that would have eventually risen the cost of bank funding) upon the introduction of the *bail-in* regime.

Hence, our dataset contains information regarding the main characteristics of the bank bonds, namely the 'yield to maturity' at launch, the 'maximum issue amount' (i.e., the amount that a bank would preferably like to raise), the 'total amount of the offer' (i.e., the amount actually collected), the 'coverage ratio' (i.e., a ratio between the 'total amount of the offer' and the 'maximum issue amount', which gives an idea of the ability of the bank in raising the greater amount desirable of debt financing), the 'maturity' of the issuance, and a *dummy* that equals one when a bond has been listed and zero otherwise.

In addition, we link to each bond issuance the yield to maturity offered by the Italian Government bonds with similar maturity.[9] In this way, we are able to generate a key variable for our analysis, that

[8]See also Chap. 2 for an analysis of Italian banks funding strategies.

[9]To this purpose we employ the so called "Rendistato"—provided by the Italian central bank (Bank of Italy)—which is the weighted average yield on a basket of Government securities, provided for different maturities. More information is available at the following link: https://www.bancaditalia.it/compiti/operazioni-mef/rendistato-rendiob/index.html?com.dotmarketing.htmlpage.language=1.

is the 'spread', namely the difference between the bank bond and the Government bond yields. Such variable—which reflects investors' perceptions about the bank's credit risk (see, inter alia, Sironi 2003)—should, at least theoretically, represent the risk premium demanded by retail investors to allocate their savings towards a bank security.

It is worthy of note that, more frequently during the first months of our sample period, the 'spread' variable also took negative values with a minimum of 3.14% (see Table 4.2). This sounds a bit odd for the theory that, instead, postulates that Government bonds should be perceived, by investors, as risk free securities—thus representing a benchmark when pricing non-Government bonds. However, such a phenomenon (i.e., the negative spread) is not new in the literature. Indeed, other researchers (see, among others, Grasso et al. 2010; Belcredi et al. 2011; Del Giudice 2016)—although on different samples and time periods—have found evidence of negative 'spread'—thus violating the agents' rationality assumption—attributable to the stronger bargaining power of banks as well as to the ability of their branches in placing own bonds (see, for instance, Belcredi et al. 2011).[10]

We now offer summary statistics related to the features of the bonds in our sample. Notably, Panel A of Table 4.2 reports the statistics of the whole sample. In Panel B, instead, we provide descriptive statistics for two different subsamples, namely a subsample of observations falling in the 'pre bail-in' period (i.e., the period before the implementation of the new regime) and a subsample of observations related to issuances made during the 'post bail-in' period (i.e., from 1 January 2016 onwards).

Interestingly, we observe that the average spread offered by the banks during the whole period is about 45 basis points, compared to the Italian Government bonds. More specifically, before the entry into force of the BRRD in Italian legislation, the average spread was about 42 basis points. After 1 January 2016 (date of implementation of the new regulation), the average spread significantly increases of almost 18 basis points (which is not a minor increase, given that it reflects an upsurge of

[10]See also, in this regard, the considerations provided in Chaps. 2 and 3.

Table 4.2 Summary statistics

	Obs.	Mean	Median	St. Deviation	Min	Max
Panel A						
Spread (%)	1,160	0.451	0.435	0.792	−3.411	5.118
Maturity (years)	1,160	4.277	3.000	2.472	1.500	25.500
Listed (dummy)	1,160	0.275	0.000	0.447	0.000	1.000
Total amount of the offer (thousand of €)	1,139	93,456	20,000	272,841	9	5,500,000
Maximum issue amount (thousand of €)	1,032	135,000,000	50,000,000	653,000,000	10,000	20,000,000,000
Coverage ratio	1,011	0.020	0.001	0.141	0.000	2.000
Panel B						
Pre bail-in period (2013–2015)						
Spread (%)	988	0.424	0.402	0.809	−3.411	4.151
Maturity (years)	988	4.266	3.000	2.379	1.500	20.000
Listed (dummy)	988	0.275	0.000	0.447	0.000	1.000
Total amount of the offer (thousand of €)	968	92,494	20,000	280,411	10	5,500,000
Maximum issue amount (thousand of €)	876	136,000,000	46,900,000	703,000,000	10,000	20,000,000,000
Coverage ratio	856	0.022	0.001	0.149	0.000	2.000
Post bail-in period (2016)						
Spread (%)	172	0.603	0.515	0.668	−1.259	5.118
Maturity (years)	172	4.343	3.000	2.957	2.000	25.500
Listed (dummy)	172	0.273	0.000	0.447	0.000	1.000
Total amount of the offer (thousand of €)	171	98,903	15,550	225,885	9	1,491,474
Maximum issue amount (thousand of €)	156	126,000,000	50,000,000	214,000,000	20,000	1,500,000,000
Coverage ratio	155	0.008	0.001	0.081	0.000	1.000

roughly 40% compared to the previous period), namely up to 60 basis points.[11]

This result is not inconsequential as it provides a noteworthy evidence of the increase in the yields offered by Italian banks, on their bonds, upon the entry into force of the BRRD in Italian legislation. The motivations behind such a rise may be the following two. First, banks might have been induced to offer greater yields in order to regain investors' confidence, which widely collapsed when bondholders were forced to cover the losses of four Italian banks under resolution in late 2015 (see next Sect. 4.5). Second, and more broadly, because with the new regime creditors are explicitly exposed to losses (i.e., in principle there would not be Government support for failing banks anymore, as the *bail-out* should be definitely excluded), banks in search of new funding might be induced to make their bonds more attractive by offering greater returns.

However, the data at our disposal does not allow us to carry out a more precise investigation of the causes behind the observed phenomenon. Indeed, linking data from banks' balance sheets and, ideally, conducting a survey to the bankers involved in the decision process of issuing new debt financing would represent valuable assets for such a study. Addressing these limitations may lay the ground for future research.

It is also worth noting that such an increase in the cost borne by the banks for their funding has an important side effect. As it is common knowledge, banks look for the maximization of their net interest margins (i.e., the difference between interest revenues minus interest expenses). Therefore, a surge in the bank's costs (due, for instance, to the need of increasing bank bonds' attractiveness) may eventually translate into higher spreads charged on loans (which represent the main source of revenues for commercial banks).

In other words, banks might shift to their borrowers the rise in the costs experienced upon the entry into force of the BRRD. This is not

[11]Unreported t-tests show that the two subsample means, of our 'spread' variable, are statistically different.

inconsequential, provided that it may result, for instance, in a further penalization for SMEs, that already suffered the credit crunch occurred during the global financial crisis (see, inter alia, Carbo-Valverde et al. 2015; Popov and Van Horen 2015; Tayler and Zilberman 2016). And this, in turn, would also have a significant impact on the real economy, provided that SMEs dominate the business scene in the EU (see, for instance, Carbo-Valverde et al. 2015; EIF 2017).

In any case, such an effect is not yet evident, considering the current environment characterized by low interest rates (due to the expansionary monetary policies of the ECB). Moreover, data from ABI (the Association of Italian banks) highlight that interest rates charged on loans have been declining so far. However, what we observe in Italy is an increase in the fares of the fee-based banking services—which might be actually the way that banks employed to shift to their customers the costs involved with the compliance to the increasingly tougher regulations.

Moving to the other rows of Table 4.2, interesting insights come also from the statistics related to the remaining bonds' characteristics. For instance, we observe that the mean of the 'coverage ratio' is very low and about 2% across the observed period, thus implying that banks found it difficult to issue the desirable amount of bonds. This might also be due to the fact that, during the last years, retail investors in Italy—most likely driven by their financial advisors—have increasingly preferred the investment in mutual funds rather than in bank bonds, for the purpose of a better diversification.[12]

As regards the maturity, we observe that on average banks issue medium-term bonds. Indeed, the mean of 'maturity' is approximately four years and three months. Finally, we note that only 27% of the bonds in our sample are listed in a market.

---

[12]See also Chap. 2.

4.5 The New Approach to Bank Resolution After the Introduction of the BRRD—*Case Studies*

Unlike other countries, Italian banks did not face big troubles during the very first wave of the financial crisis—mainly due to their limited exposure to American sub-prime securities, but also because Italy did not experience a housing bubble like Spain for instance. However, criticalities within the Italian banking industry started to appear after the blast of the Euro area sovereign debt crisis in 2010, which led to a deep recession of the Italian economy with an increasing number of firms facing severe problems and, eventually, shutting down. This, in turn, caused deteriorations in banks' assets given the sharp increase in the share of non-performing loans (NPLs). As of 2016, non-performing loans amounted to 360 billion Euros (gross figure). Additionally, more than two thirds of the bad loans are to non-financial SMEs.[13]

Despite the worrisome state of the art, no actions were taken to carry out a decisive restructuring process like the ones implemented in countries under the IMF assistance. This led to concerns, late in 2015, about the possible threats that the banking industry and retail investors might face upon the entry into force of the BRRD along with the unsettled NPL problems. Indeed, from the banks' liabilities side, a substantial share of debt issued via junior bonds is held by retail investors. Data from Bank of Italy (2016) show that at the end of 2015 the exposure of Italian households to subordinated bank bonds was almost 30 billion Euros. Notably, 10% of Italian savers' financial assets was in *bail-inable* instruments,[14] with subordinated bonds covering 1% of such exposure (see, in this regard, Philippon and Salord 2017). At first glance, this modest figure may not be particularly worrying. However, lots of those risky bonds were in households' portfolios. Indeed, as reported by

---

[13]Note that the greater shares of NPLs are recorded in the Southern regions where the economic context has been critical since ages.

[14]*Bail-inable* instruments mainly include subordinated bonds, senior unsecured bonds, and deposits above the 100,000 Euros threshold.

Grasso et al. (2010), from the second half of 2007 to the first half of 2009, Italian banks placed 80% of their bonds[15] to retail investors—who, most likely unconsciously (i.e., underestimating or not understanding the risks they were going to be exposed to), invested their savings to buy them.[16]

The first critical episode came out in November 2015, when the Italian Resolution Authority decided to resolve four small or medium-sized banks, namely: **Banca delle Marche**, **Banca Popolare dell'Etruria e del Lazio**, **Cassa di Risparmio della Provincia di Chieti**, and **Cassa di Risparmio di Ferrara.**[17] The Resolution Authority implemented a burden-sharing mechanism (that is a 'quasi' *bail-in*) just some weeks before the BRRD officially entered into force in January 2016. Initially, the idea was to implement a sort of private *bail-out* by accessing sources from the 'Fondo Interbancario di Tutela dei Depositi' (FITD), an Italian deposit guarantee scheme funded by all Italian banks except for the cooperative ones that have their own scheme.[18] However, the DG COMP[19] rejected the proposed plan (that did not comply with state aid rules) thus imposing resolution—which basically consists in the restructuring of a bank—and a partial *bail-in*. Therefore, losses were absorbed by shareholders and subordinated creditors. Then, a 'bad' bank (i.e., an asset management vehicle) was created to allocate all the problematic assets (mainly NPLs). The original four banks, instead, technically became a bridge institution (i.e., 'good' bank) each, and overall were refilled of equity to 9% by the

[15]It is worth mentioning that issuing junior bonds was an easy way, for Italian banks, to get funded at lower rates during the financial crisis—a period characterized by heavy liquidity shortages (see, for instance, Cingano et al. 2016).

[16]See also Chap. 2 in this regard.

[17]These banks accounted for about 1% of the Italian banking system; see, for instance, Bank of Italy (2015).

[18]Note that the deposit insurance schemes in Italy are not funded with money from the Government; rather they collect contributions from their members.

[19]DG COMP is the acronym of "Directorate-General for Competition", a Body of the European Commission that is responsible for implementing a coherent competition policy—under the framework of the so-called state aid rules—within the European Union common market.

Italian Resolution Fund.[20] The Fund also provided guarantees to the 'bad' bank. The total contribution from the Resolution Fund is estimated in 3.6 billion Euros; these resources were used for the absorption of remaining losses from the original banks, for recapitalization of the bridge banks, as well as for capital injection to the 'bad' bank (see, in this regard, World Bank Group 2016b).[21]

Overall, this story sheds light on how challenging could be implementing resolutions in Italy. From one side there is a forward-looking and noble act of avoiding that the costs of future bank rescues are borne by taxpayers—which is also reasonable for Italy that has an already high level of sovereign debt. From the other side, instead, there is a crowd of retail investors that would possibly need to be safeguarded, provided that they very likely purchased subordinated bonds without clear consciousness of the risks characterizing such instruments. In this regard, it is worth noting that one of the criticisms of the BRRD—commonly raised by practitioners as well as by politicians—relates to the retroactivity of its implementation (see, in this regard, Boccuzzi and De Lisa 2017). Indeed, it looks quite unfair—for those who (consciously or not) filled their portfolios with risky bonds during a *bail-out* regime—to find out that the rules have changed during the game.

Ideally, policy makers and financial Authorities (Consob and Banca of Italy) should have better monitored banks, thus to induce them not to issue junior debt to retail investors. This would have also avoided extreme acts such as the one of a pensioner who killed himself when he found out that his 100,000 Euros savings (invested in Banca Popolare dell'Etruria e del Lazio subordinated bonds) were completely

---

[20]Interestingly, the four "good banks" were later sold for just one euro each to UBI Banking Group and BPER.

[21]The Italian Resolution Fund is funded (via ex-ante contributions) through sources from the Italian banking industry. Provided that the Fund did not have enough sources for the resolution of the four banks (as it was only recently settled), in order to avoid an intervention by the Italian Government—as the *bail-out* was no longer possible—the required sources were anticipated by three of the largest Italian banks (i.e., Unicredit, Intesa Sanpaolo, and Unione di Banche Italiane). Therefore, in 2015 the ex-ante (ordinary) contributions amounted to 588 million Euros, whereas the extra contributions from the three large banks reached 175 billion of Euros.

lost (Philippon and Salord 2017).[22] To curb the occurrence of similar events, in May 2016 the Italian legislator passed a law to partly refund (naïve) retail investors of the four resolved banks.

The case just described was the first one in which a sort of *bail-in* rescue was implemented in Italy. Probably, it received a considerable attention by national and international mass media because it involved four banks at the same time.[23] Indeed, the news of the 'quasi *bail-in*' applied to those small and regionally chartered banks became the hot topic, for a while, in TVs, newspapers, and social media as well. This led Italians, at least for a while, to credibly think that the *bail-out* regime was definitely suppressed.

However, in June 2017 Italian investors and depositors may have felt a bit disoriented when they heard the news of a 17 billion Euros Government support in favour of **Banca Popolare di Vicenza** and **Veneto Banca.**[24] These two banks had a strong presence in the North-Eastern provinces of the Boot and accounted for about 2% of the Italian banking system.[25]

In essence, the Italian Government found the proper way to convince DG COMP—probably leveraging on the financial instability that a liquidation without any state support for those two small or medium-sized

[22]The news received great attention worldwide. See, for instance, 'Italy bank rescue marred by suicide and lost savings', BBC, December 10, 2015, available at: http://www.bbc.com/news/world-europe-35062239.

[23]For the sake of precision, a preceding rescue occurred in Italy in July 2015 with the liquidation of Banca Romagna Cooperativa (BRC). However, this episode was almost disregarded, probably because retail bondholders did not suffered any loss thanks to the refund they received from the "Fondo di Garanzia Istituzionale", which is the Deposit Insurance Scheme financed by Italian cooperative banks (World Bank Group 2016b).

[24]State aid was approved by the European Commission on June 25, 2017, to facilitate the liquidation of the two banks. Indeed, such a decision followed the announcement of the ECB that the two banks were failing or likely to fail (FOLTF), and the subsequent decision by the SRB that there was no public interest in resolving the two banks. See the official press release by the European Commission at the following link: http://europa.eu/rapid/press-release_IP-17-1791_en.htm.

[25]Criticisms on this issue were raised by foreign media. See, for instance, 'Italy's Latest Bank Bailout Has Created A Two-Speed Eurozone', Forbes, June 26, 2017, available at: https://www.forbes.com/sites/francescoppola/2017/06/26/italys-latest-bank-bailout-has-created-a-two-speed-eurozone/#6424086144a4.

banks would have generated—that it was better to avoid a heavy *bail-in* rescue.[26]

Indeed, it is a politicians' interest to prevent the possible discontent that would arise when savers (i.e., bondholders and, finally, depositors) are wiped out after a severe resolution decision is taken.

In addition, some days later the market could finally see the end of **Monte dei Paschi di Siena** saga, the fourteenth century monolith and currently fifth largest Italian bank that experienced a never-ending negotiation, about its destiny, between the European Commission and the Italian Government. Eventually, Brussels and Rome sealed an agreement early in July 2017, which involves a 'precautionary recapitalization'—an option provided by the BRRD for solvent banks in order to ensure their long-term viability—with 5.4 billion Euros of state aid. For the sake of precision note that, for a 'precautionary recapitalization' to take place, a prior 'burden-sharing' is needed. Indeed, shareholders and junior creditors contributed with 4.3 billion Euros before the capital injection was approved.[27] Overall, in less than a month, taxpayers in Italy contributed with more than 20 billion Euros to support the Italian banking industry.

The case studies illustrated above leave us with an interesting food for thought. What we understand is that Governments face the following trade-off. From one side, there is the need to avoid the unfair practise of mutualizing the losses (due to bad management) occurred at a privately owned financial institution with all taxpayers (that actually do not share any interest with the failing institution)—along with the

[26]Indeed, the European Commission approved, under EU rules, Italian measures to facilitate the liquidation of Banca Popolare di Vicenza and Veneto Banca under national insolvency law. These measures involved the sale of some of the two banks' businesses (for the token price of 1 Euro) to be integrated into Intesa Sanpaolo.

[27]State aid in the form of capital injection was authorized on July 4, 2017. See the official press release by the European Commission at the following link: http://europa.eu/rapid/press-release_IP-17-1905_en.htm.

consequent rise in a country's public debt. And this represents an ideal forward-looking policy.[28] However, from the other side, politicians—who typically act with a short-term focus (as their goal is winning the following electoral competition)—are generally more willing to contain their voters' anger by doing all their best—hence including the use of public money—to avoid them incurring in losses.

Apart from such a questionable consideration, the truth is somewhere in between. Namely, we think that it is not realistic to achieve resolutions, recapitalizations and liquidations without public support in every possible case.[29] Indeed, one needs always to keep in mind that not all of a bank's creditors should be placed in the same line. Put it differently, among the bondholders there might also be simple savers who ended up with investing their all life savings in *bail-inable* instruments as a result of the bank's persuasion—and this was actually the case of the vast majority of subordinated bondholders of the four small banks resolved in December 2015 in Italy.[30]

Nonetheless, we are also aware that 'easy' *bail-outs*, as the ones readily carried out in the aftermath of the global financial crisis, are not feasible anymore. Indeed, restructuring plans are far better than state aids, which ultimately contribute to create 'zombie' banks with significant costs for the state coffers and the economy as a whole (Reichlin 2017).

4.6 Conclusions

After having highlighted the main features of the BRRD, we have provided the reader with a detailed description of the *bail-in* tool, which characterizes the new approach to bank resolutions.

---

[28] And, obviously, it is in line with the scope of the BRRD.

[29] And, in fact, the BRRD itself allows a government intervention as a last resort possibility. Moreover, the BRRD framework is forcing banks to have a sufficient amount of *bail-inable* instruments (MREL). In this regard, see also Chap. 1.

[30] In this regard, however, we hope that the new rules introduced by MiFID II about Product Governance will avoid, in the future, such unfair and misleading type of selling.

The analysis carried out in this Chapter—through the use of data from a unique hand-collected dataset—underscored that, since the adoption of the BRRD in the European Union, Italian banks have been forced to offer higher yields (compared to the yields offered by government securities with corresponding maturities) to bondholders, with the consequent side-effect of an increase in their cost of funding. Such a rise in the bonds' *spread* may be motivated by the need of banks to increase the appeal of their debt instruments that has been heavily damaged by the acquired awareness that—upon the implementation of the BRRD—savers might be likely to bear losses in case of failure.

Finally, we have concluded our final Chapter by offering some very recent examples about the application of the BRDD rules in Italy—which have either led to liquidation, resolution, or precautionary recapitalization cases—and the related side effects generated to bank bondholders.

References

Arnaboldi, F., 2014. Deposit Guarantee Schemes. A European Perspective. Palgrave Macmillan, London.

Bank of Italy, 2015. Information on resolution of Banca Marche, Banca Popolare dell'Etruria e del Lazio, Carichieti, and Cassa di Risparmio di Ferrara crises. Available at: https://www.bancaditalia.it/media/approfondimenti/2015/info-soluzione-crisi/info-banche-en.pdf?language_id=1.

Bank of Italy, 2016. Financial Stability Report No. 1, Rome.

Belcredi, M., Croci, E., Del Giudice, A., 2011. Il silenzio degli agnelli. Risparmiatori e obbligazioni bancarie in Italia. Mercato concorrenza regole XIII, 93–116.

Benczur, P., Cannas, G., Cariboni, J., Di Girolamo, F., Maccaferri, S., Petracco Giudici, M., 2016. Evaluating the effectiveness of the new EU bank regulatory framework: A farewell to bail-out? Journal of Financial Stability, forthcoming. http://dx.doi.org/10.1016/j.jfs.2016.03.001.

Boccuzzi, G., De Lisa, R., 2017. Does bail-in definitely rule out bailout? Journal of Financial Management, Markets and Institutions 5 (1), 93–110.

Bufacchi, I., 2017. Italian banks moving fast to reduce bonds sold to customers. Italy Europe 24, January 23. Available at: http://www.italy24.ilsole24ore.com/print/AEYpIpE/0.

Carbo-Valverde, S., Degryse, H., Rodríguez-Fernández, F., 2015. The impact of securitization on credit rationing: Empirical evidence. Journal of Financial Stability 20, 36–50.
Cingano, F., Manaresi, F., Sette, E., 2016. Does credit crunch investment down? New evidence on the real effects of the bank-lending channel. The Review of Financial Studies 29 (10), 2737–2773.
Coletta, M., Santioni, R., 2016. Le obbligazioni bancarie nel portafoglio delle famiglie italiane. Questioni di Economia e Finanza (Occasional papers) No. 359, Banca d'Italia.
Del Giudice, A., 2016. Impact of the Market in Financial Instruments Directive (MiFID) on the Italian financial market: Evidence from bank bonds. Journal of Banking Regulation. doi:10.1057/s41261-016-0035-7.
ECB, 2016. Systemic implications of the European bail-in tool: A multi-layered network analysis. Financial Stability Review, May. Frankfurt.
ECB, 2017. Who supervises my bank? Available at: https://www.bankingsupervision.europa.eu/banking/list/who/html/index.en.html.
EIF, 2017. European Small Business Finance Outlook. Working Paper No. 43.
Grasso, R., Linciano, N., Pierantoni, L., Siciliano, G., 2010. Bonds issued by Italian banks. Risk and return characteristics. Consob Working Paper No. 67.
Hüser, A.-C., Hałaj, G., Kok, C., Perales, C., van der Kraaij, A., 2017. The systemic implications of bail-in: a multi-layered network approach. ECB Working Paper Series, 2010.
Peia, O., Vranceanu, R., 2017. Experimental evidence on bank runs under partial deposit insurance. Working Paper No. 1705. Essec Business School.
Philippon, T., Salord, A., 2017. Bail-ins and Bank Resolution in Europe: A progress report. Geneva Reports on the World Economy Special Report 4. International Center for Monetary and Banking Studies (ICMB), Geneva (Switzerland); Centre for Economic Policy Research (CEPR), London (UK).
Popov, A., Van Horen, N., 2015. Exporting Sovereign Stress: Evidence from Syndicated Bank Lending During the Euro Area Sovereign Debt Crisis. Review of Finance 19, 1825–1866.
Reichlin, L., 2017. The European banking union falls short in Italy. Veneto brings a lesson on how to deal with failing banks. Financial Times, June 27. Available at: https://www.ft.com/content/3b8bc570-5a7e-11e7-b553-e2df1b0c3220.
Sironi, A., 2003. Testing for market discipline in the European banking industry: Evidence from subordinated debt issues. Journal of Money, Credit and Banking 35 (3), 443–472.
SRB, 2017. Single Resolution Board. Annual Report 2016. Publications Office of the European Union, Luxembourg.

Tayler, W.J., Zilberman, R., 2016. Macroprudential regulation, credit spreads and the role of monetary policy. Journal of Financial Stability 26, 144–158.
Ueda, K. and Weder di Mauro, B., 2013. Quantifying structural subsidy values for systemically important financial institutions. Journal of Banking & Finance 37 (10), 3830–3842.
World Bank Group, 2016a. Understanding bank recovery and resolution in the EU: A guidebook to the BRRD. Financial Sector Advisory Center (FinSAC), Vienna (Austria).
World Bank Group, 2016b. Bank resolution and "Bail-in" in the EU: Selected case studies pre and post BRRD. Financial Sector Advisory Center (FinSAC), Vienna (Austria).
Zaghini, A., 2014. Bank bonds: Size, systemic relevance and the sovereign. International Finance 17 (2), 161–183.

Conclusions

The analysis carried out throughout the chapters of this monograph has highlighted the deep evolution that banks have experienced in terms of their funding strategies during the last ten years. As we pointed out, the last decade has been characterized by remarkable events (i.e., two major financial crises) that have heavily affected the stability of the financial systems and the real economy as well.

In light of such circumstances, the policy makers' response has translated into tougher regulation for banks (Basel III) and limited participation of taxpayers to banks' defaults (i.e., from *bail-out* to *bail-in*). The effects generated by the crises on the real economy (low GDP growth, high levels of non-performing loans, high money in circulation, low interest rates and so on), along with the important regulatory changes meanwhile adopted, have surely affected the behaviour of European banks in regards to their approach towards funding, as well as towards the management of their assets.

Overall, our broader analysis on the largest European economies has shown the increasing importance of retail deposits as the main funding instrument used by credit institutions (especially to replace wholesale funding, strongly used before the crisis), as well as a remarkable contraction of the share of bonds issued in the last few years.

F. Crespi and D. V. Mascia, *Bank Funding Strategies*, Palgrave Macmillan Studies in Banking and Financial Institutions, https://doi.org/10.1007/978-3-319-69413-9

Data from the Italian banking industry confirm these trends and highlight a severe contraction in the bank bonds issuances since 2013. In addition, the data underscore that—given the compliance to the new rules discouraging the issuance of complex products—over the recent years banks have mainly issued plain vanilla (unlisted) bonds. Moreover, our analysis pointed out how, in the past, a certain opacity of the banking industry led to the dissemination of important amounts of risky bonds to unconscious savers. These evidences considerably came out soon after the decision of resolving four small banks in November 2015, when a significant number of Italian savers—holding subordinated bonds of these banks—were forced by the Resolution Authority to share the burden of the banks' losses, losing in many cases a vast amount of their all life savings. This news had a great resonance in the media and panic effect was easily spread among depositors, who actually transferred much of their deposits from failing or suspected weak banks to strongest ones.

Additionally, our analysis has highlighted that—since the adoption of the BRRD in the European Union—Italian banks have been forced to offer higher yields (compared to the yields offered by government securities with corresponding maturities) to bondholders, with the consequent side-effect of an increase in their cost of funding. Such a rise in the bonds' *spread* may be motivated by the need of banks to increase the appeal of their debt instruments that has been heavily damaged by the acquired awareness that—upon the implementation of the BRRD—savers might be likely to bear losses in case of failure.

Finally, it is worthy of note that the decline in the share of bonds—compared to the overall banks' liabilities—observed over the recent years does not exclude that, in the future, banks will turn again to significantly use these debt instruments. Indeed, financial institutions might be likely to increase the weight of their bonds within their liabilities if an improvement of the macroeconomic conditions—along with an overall rise of interest rates—would make bonds more appealing for retail investors and more favourable for banks as a long-term source of funding.

Appendices A1 and A2

F. Crespi and D. V. Mascia, *Bank Funding Strategies*, Palgrave Macmillan Studies in Banking and Financial Institutions, https://doi.org/10.1007/978-3-319-69413-9

Table A1 Data gathered from the statistical database ("Base Dati Statistica", BDS), available at Bank of Italy, along with authors' calculations

Date	Loans to residents	Deposits of residents	Bonds issued	Other liabilities	Total Liabilities (Deposits + Bonds + Others)	Equity	Total liabilities and equity = Total assets	Loans to Total Assets	Loans to Deposits	Deposits over liabilities	Bonds over liabili-ties	Other liabilities over liabilities	Equity over Total Assets
31/01/99	882,454.32	687,194.54	251,157.05	550,107.75	1,488,459.34	110,458.52	1,598,917.86	0.55	1.28	0.46	0.17	0.37	0.07
28/02/99	877,602.62	687,029.29	254,315.52	521,533.62	1,462,878.43	110,496.60	1,573,375.03	0.56	1.28	0.47	0.17	0.36	0.07
31/03/99	876,513.66	667,967.64	256,560.43	510,883.11	1,435,411.18	111,101.52	1,546,512.70	0.57	1.31	0.47	0.18	0.36	0.07
30/04/99	886,808.68	679,731.84	258,517.63	510,120.30	1,448,369.77	112,136.83	1,560,506.60	0.57	1.30	0.47	0.18	0.35	0.07
31/05/99	896,953.22	685,166.21	261,715.39	511,373.94	1,458,255.54	112,780.87	1,571,036.41	0.57	1.31	0.47	0.18	0.35	0.07
30/06/99	930,650.98	707,519.24	263,757.94	526,356.56	1,497,633.74	115,073.81	1,612,707.55	0.58	1.32	0.47	0.18	0.35	0.07
31/07/99	918,184.26	687,431.90	263,247.40	512,342.68	1,463,021.98	115,160.76	1,578,182.74	0.58	1.34	0.47	0.18	0.35	0.07
31/08/99	915,772.37	682,029.46	264,088.10	499,155.01	1,445,272.57	115,168.88	1,560,441.45	0.59	1.34	0.47	0.18	0.35	0.07
30/09/99	919,785.70	684,689.36	264,552.55	498,724.81	1,447,966.72	115,178.55	1,563,145.27	0.59	1.34	0.47	0.18	0.34	0.07
31/10/99	926,532.30	688,527.09	266,438.31	512,376.27	1,467,341.67	114,595.86	1,581,937.53	0.59	1.35	0.47	0.18	0.35	0.07
30/11/99	953,837.66	674,652.49	269,808.10	549,047.77	1,493,508.36	114,581.47	1,608,089.83	0.59	1.41	0.45	0.18	0.37	0.07
31/12/99	979,237.34	730,578.88	271,553.24	508,407.22	1,510,539.34	118,264.80	1,628,804.14	0.60	1.34	0.48	0.18	0.34	0.07
31/01/00	990,410.08	719,685.61	273,806.46	542,616.10	1,536,108.17	121,672.33	1,657,780.50	0.60	1.38	0.47	0.18	0.35	0.07
29/02/00	998,259.93	723,486.78	277,720.52	537,031.38	1,538,238.68	123,734.85	1,661,973.53	0.60	1.38	0.47	0.18	0.35	0.07
31/03/00	1,011,013.05	733,454.15	284,381.43	547,188.90	1,565,024.48	124,822.68	1,689,847.16	0.60	1.38	0.47	0.18	0.35	0.07
30/04/00	1,013,689.18	745,012.35	286,331.54	544,441.17	1,575,785.06	126,076.43	1,701,861.49	0.60	1.36	0.47	0.18	0.35	0.07
31/05/00	1,024,134.18	758,685.74	288,065.66	546,891.69	1,593,643.09	126,583.55	1,720,226.64	0.60	1.35	0.48	0.18	0.34	0.07
30/06/00	1,056,056.63	767,117.97	289,153.57	548,040.37	1,604,311.91	126,530.15	1,730,842.06	0.61	1.38	0.48	0.18	0.34	0.07
31/07/00	1,050,404.72	750,865.98	288,143.57	540,567.46	1,579,577.01	127,259.88	1,706,836.89	0.62	1.40	0.48	0.18	0.34	0.07
31/08/00	1,042,597.57	729,930.98	289,957.08	539,926.93	1,559,814.99	127,368.80	1,687,183.79	0.62	1.43	0.47	0.19	0.35	0.08
30/09/00	1,048,595.50	725,295.77	293,992.05	561,898.16	1,581,185.98	127,652.61	1,708,838.59	0.61	1.45	0.46	0.19	0.36	0.07
31/10/00	1,071,828.38	737,063.09	294,624.11	592,189.55	1,623,876.75	127,543.00	1,751,419.75	0.61	1.45	0.45	0.18	0.36	0.07
30/11/00	1,096,563.90	735,917.56	296,669.55	602,415.91	1,635,003.02	127,761.18	1,762,764.20	0.62	1.49	0.45	0.18	0.37	0.07
31/12/00	1,110,507.26	775,475.06	302,480.77	569,240.15	1,647,195.98	123,930.00	1,771,125.98	0.63	1.43	0.47	0.18	0.35	0.07
31/01/01	1,090,326.32	729,791.45	302,741.78	578,412.61	1,610,945.84	125,840.78	1,736,786.62	0.63	1.49	0.45	0.19	0.36	0.07
28/02/01	1,081,582.26	718,855.93	306,752.77	577,139.33	1,602,748.03	126,790.39	1,729,538.42	0.63	1.50	0.45	0.19	0.36	0.07
31/03/01	1,108,247.08	742,904.12	312,612.48	612,146.26	1,667,662.86	128,430.41	1,796,093.27	0.62	1.49	0.45	0.19	0.37	0.07
30/04/01	1,112,823.39	733,509.65	314,992.20	611,117.52	1,659,619.37	131,997.39	1,791,616.76	0.62	1.52	0.44	0.19	0.37	0.07
31/05/01	1,115,482.97	760,528.40	316,901.26	592,050.09	1,669,479.75	130,071.38	1,799,551.13	0.62	1.47	0.46	0.19	0.35	0.07
30/06/01	1,136,973.14	763,072.32	319,911.22	605,615.94	1,688,599.48	131,744.81	1,820,344.29	0.62	1.49	0.45	0.19	0.36	0.07
31/07/01	1,142,113.73	756,888.40	322,814.57	590,492.37	1,670,195.34	131,991.90	1,802,187.24	0.63	1.51	0.45	0.19	0.35	0.07
31/08/01	1,130,717.34	753,462.81	325,303.31	562,849.56	1,641,615.68	132,553.53	1,774,169.21	0.64	1.50	0.46	0.20	0.34	0.07

(continued)

Table A1 (continued)

Date	Loans to residents	Deposits of residents	Bonds issued	Other liabilities	Total Liabilities (Deposits + Bonds + Others)	Equity	Total liabilities and equity = Total assets	Loans to Total Assets	Loans to Deposits	Deposits over liabilities	Bonds over liabilities	Other liabilities over liabilities	Equity over Total Assets
30/09/01	1,139,810.04	762,320.46	327,487.94	584,094.58	1,673,902.98	132,584.35	1,806,487.33	0.63	1.50	0.46	0.20	0.35	0.07
31/10/01	1,145,141.35	769,170.75	327,829.15	584,671.35	1,681,671.25	133,015.44	1,814,686.69	0.63	1.49	0.46	0.19	0.35	0.07
30/11/01	1,176,688.70	769,853.79	331,111.04	612,883.89	1,713,848.72	133,071.53	1,846,920.25	0.64	1.53	0.45	0.19	0.36	0.07
31/12/01	1,185,653.67	798,483.04	334,672.35	585,202.11	1,718,357.50	133,633.20	1,851,990.70	0.64	1.48	0.46	0.19	0.34	0.07
31/01/02	1,162,891.92	771,708.93	336,452.75	611,722.09	1,719,883.77	136,122.74	1,856,006.51	0.63	1.51	0.45	0.20	0.36	0.07
28/02/02	1,161,296.79	778,303.99	340,214.22	580,480.07	1,698,998.28	136,181.26	1,835,179.54	0.63	1.49	0.46	0.20	0.34	0.07
31/03/02	1,178,645.67	799,741.74	344,767.80	584,057.94	1,728,567.48	136,712.27	1,865,279.75	0.63	1.47	0.46	0.20	0.34	0.07
30/04/02	1,184,881.79	810,242.84	347,323.95	582,521.57	1,740,088.36	138,215.78	1,878,304.14	0.63	1.46	0.47	0.20	0.33	0.07
31/05/02	1,205,715.04	826,881.10	352,295.99	573,678.30	1,752,855.39	138,183.08	1,891,038.47	0.64	1.46	0.47	0.20	0.33	0.07
30/06/02	1,199,399.03	817,198.08	358,665.95	569,983.54	1,745,847.57	138,908.92	1,884,756.49	0.64	1.47	0.47	0.21	0.33	0.07
31/07/02	1,227,639.86	835,232.26	357,820.86	571,452.09	1,764,505.21	145,747.20	1,910,252.41	0.64	1.47	0.47	0.20	0.32	0.08
31/08/02	1,224,361.86	832,024.61	359,830.19	549,526.04	1,741,380.84	145,718.98	1,887,099.82	0.65	1.47	0.48	0.21	0.32	0.08
30/09/02	1,225,002.43	838,575.45	362,979.95	553,006.52	1,754,561.92	146,215.53	1,900,777.45	0.64	1.46	0.48	0.21	0.32	0.08
31/10/02	1,239,882.30	854,203.13	364,076.96	556,800.64	1,775,080.73	147,720.06	1,922,800.79	0.64	1.45	0.48	0.21	0.31	0.08
30/11/02	1,258,990.59	872,073.63	364,817.35	572,748.25	1,809,639.23	147,019.20	1,956,658.43	0.64	1.44	0.48	0.20	0.32	0.08
31/12/02	1,322,114.49	943,475.60	367,969.15	566,539.29	1,877,984.04	146,172.38	2,024,156.42	0.65	1.40	0.50	0.20	0.30	0.07
31/01/03	1,321,496.06	917,337.77	367,583.86	588,875.45	1,873,797.08	147,115.21	2,020,912.29	0.65	1.44	0.49	0.20	0.31	0.07
28/02/03	1,321,742.94	916,151.25	368,647.65	603,345.15	1,888,144.05	146,877.77	2,035,021.82	0.65	1.44	0.49	0.20	0.32	0.07
31/03/03	1,315,062.10	916,361.43	373,332.10	601,524.74	1,891,218.27	147,815.14	2,039,033.41	0.64	1.44	0.48	0.20	0.32	0.07
30/04/03	1,303,324.52	916,224.59	375,522.75	592,151.03	1,883,898.37	149,092.02	2,032,990.39	0.64	1.42	0.49	0.20	0.31	0.07
31/05/03	1,315,876.09	926,634.81	379,615.31	601,796.34	1,908,046.46	149,826.77	2,057,873.23	0.64	1.42	0.49	0.20	0.32	0.07
30/06/03	1,338,201.19	928,764.03	380,512.41	615,976.34	1,925,252.78	149,845.59	2,075,098.37	0.64	1.44	0.48	0.20	0.32	0.07
31/07/03	1,338,895.18	929,853.69	380,378.34	594,481.69	1,904,713.72	153,269.78	2,057,983.50	0.65	1.44	0.49	0.20	0.31	0.07
31/08/03	1,341,668.29	926,590.93	381,445.18	578,866.06	1,886,902.17	153,421.02	2,040,323.19	0.66	1.45	0.49	0.20	0.31	0.08
30/09/03	1,358,194.43	944,852.45	383,934.41	595,859.58	1,924,646.44	153,926.05	2,078,572.49	0.65	1.44	0.49	0.20	0.31	0.07
31/10/03	1,367,643.41	951,117.58	386,890.43	585,438.23	1,923,446.24	153,793.99	2,077,240.23	0.66	1.44	0.49	0.20	0.30	0.07
30/11/03	1,373,207.53	953,251.53	388,692.36	594,638.35	1,936,582.24	153,986.16	2,090,568.40	0.66	1.44	0.49	0.20	0.31	0.07
31/12/03	1,402,106.20	978,692.18	399,958.48	589,990.17	1,968,640.83	156,725.99	2,125,366.82	0.66	1.43	0.50	0.20	0.30	0.07
31/01/04	1,401,065.76	974,258.42	399,519.37	625,449.74	1,999,227.53	158,496.28	2,157,723.81	0.65	1.44	0.49	0.20	0.31	0.07
29/02/04	1,397,048.41	966,143.85	402,231.46	618,184.68	1,986,559.99	158,980.26	2,145,540.25	0.65	1.45	0.49	0.20	0.31	0.07
31/03/04	1,407,545.04	981,715.54	411,170.93	638,151.88	2,031,038.35	160,934.23	2,191,972.58	0.64	1.43	0.48	0.20	0.31	0.07
30/04/04	1,409,141.04	986,945.42	413,977.50	619,195.78	2,020,118.70	161,437.81	2,181,556.51	0.65	1.43	0.49	0.20	0.31	0.07
31/05/04	1,411,248.07	987,967.40	419,993.62	617,684.61	2,025,645.63	161,517.70	2,187,163.33	0.65	1.43	0.49	0.21	0.30	0.07

(continued)

Table A1 (continued)

Date	Loans to residents	Deposits of residents	Bonds issued	Other liabilities	Total Liabilities (Deposits + Bonds + Others)	Equity	Total liabilities and equity = Total assets	Loans to Total Assets	Loans to Deposits	Deposits over liabilities	Bonds over liabili-ties	Other liabilities over liabilities	Equity over Total Assets
30/06/04	1,417,428.27	983,134.24	419,267.09	626,544.83	2,028,946.16	161,630.41	2,190,576.57	0.65	1.44	0.48	0.21	0.31	0.07
31/07/04	1,438,023.11	1,001,711.54	421,826.21	610,801.74	2,034,339.49	161,468.62	2,195,808.11	0.65	1.44	0.49	0.21	0.30	0.07
31/08/04	1,434,671.16	988,777.05	423,527.08	610,230.60	2,022,534.73	161,462.68	2,183,997.41	0.66	1.45	0.49	0.21	0.30	0.07
30/09/04	1,438,874.35	998,713.02	431,000.51	612,179.35	2,041,892.88	161,669.19	2,203,562.07	0.65	1.44	0.49	0.21	0.30	0.07
31/10/04	1,441,548.02	1,016,241.71	437,176.93	607,593.07	2,061,011.71	161,854.47	2,222,866.18	0.65	1.42	0.49	0.21	0.29	0.07
30/11/04	1,454,692.41	999,432.84	438,181.07	663,818.98	2,101,432.89	162,393.97	2,263,826.86	0.64	1.46	0.48	0.21	0.32	0.07
31/12/04	1,487,979.14	1,037,836.07	442,994.10	631,618.50	2,112,448.67	163,181.11	2,275,629.78	0.65	1.43	0.49	0.21	0.30	0.07
31/01/05	1,496,391.54	1,021,883.69	442,681.83	660,897.71	2,125,463.23	165,153.93	2,290,617.16	0.65	1.46	0.48	0.21	0.31	0.07
28/02/05	1,489,041.61	1,012,558.40	451,423.28	662,695.84	2,126,677.52	165,142.07	2,291,819.59	0.65	1.47	0.48	0.21	0.31	0.07
31/03/05	1,503,471.82	1,029,665.55	458,198.32	674,800.93	2,162,664.80	166,902.94	2,329,567.74	0.65	1.46	0.48	0.21	0.31	0.07
30/04/05	1,509,669.09	1,043,459.26	460,336.67	683,446.23	2,187,242.16	168,748.69	2,355,990.85	0.64	1.45	0.48	0.21	0.31	0.07
31/05/05	1,533,826.17	1,072,967.89	464,568.81	709,378.85	2,246,915.55	170,435.89	2,417,351.44	0.63	1.43	0.48	0.21	0.32	0.07
30/06/05	1,559,151.43	1,083,225.52	471,047.41	719,413.21	2,273,686.14	171,244.05	2,444,930.19	0.64	1.44	0.48	0.21	0.32	0.07
31/07/05	1,549,545.64	1,074,468.65	470,169.02	699,426.56	2,244,064.23	175,412.00	2,419,476.23	0.64	1.44	0.48	0.21	0.31	0.07
31/08/05	1,550,232.94	1,065,282.78	467,899.00	703,732.94	2,236,914.72	174,943.00	2,411,857.72	0.64	1.46	0.48	0.21	0.31	0.07
30/09/05	1,565,229.94	1,079,934.84	470,643.76	724,039.15	2,274,617.75	175,071.25	2,449,689.00	0.64	1.45	0.47	0.21	0.32	0.07
31/10/05	1,584,904.16	1,096,817.31	474,024.94	732,975.76	2,303,818.01	175,699.19	2,479,517.20	0.64	1.45	0.48	0.21	0.32	0.07
30/11/05	1,595,883.97	1,087,054.14	476,526.19	767,318.59	2,330,898.92	190,920.57	2,521,819.49	0.63	1.47	0.47	0.20	0.33	0.08
31/12/05	1,606,758.90	1,125,257.77	484,416.31	708,354.54	2,318,028.62	191,406.54	2,509,435.16	0.64	1.43	0.49	0.21	0.31	0.08
31/01/06	1,623,391.89	1,114,472.72	483,651.72	746,253.88	2,344,378.32	193,785.07	2,538,163.39	0.64	1.46	0.48	0.21	0.32	0.08
28/02/06	1,610,328.44	1,092,914.17	495,697.21	732,732.43	2,321,343.81	193,850.80	2,515,194.61	0.64	1.47	0.47	0.21	0.32	0.08
31/03/06	1,630,587.89	1,110,297.56	504,488.72	737,867.42	2,352,653.70	195,905.96	2,548,559.66	0.64	1.47	0.47	0.21	0.31	0.08
30/04/06	1,651,886.56	1,136,131.55	507,952.20	735,869.45	2,379,953.20	197,129.50	2,577,082.70	0.64	1.45	0.48	0.21	0.31	0.08
31/05/06	1,679,040.44	1,152,785.32	512,154.39	746,505.89	2,411,445.60	198,368.06	2,609,813.66	0.64	1.46	0.48	0.21	0.31	0.08
30/06/06	1,683,580.25	1,143,599.01	516,788.75	737,291.87	2,397,679.63	196,966.25	2,594,645.88	0.65	1.47	0.48	0.22	0.31	0.08
31/07/06	1,712,177.82	1,157,603.87	519,239.12	749,899.01	2,426,742.00	198,521.76	2,625,263.76	0.65	1.48	0.48	0.21	0.31	0.08
31/08/06	1,710,394.47	1,145,273.62	521,446.16	754,678.57	2,421,398.35	198,580.31	2,619,978.66	0.65	1.49	0.47	0.22	0.31	0.08
30/09/06	1,735,509.86	1,178,244.40	523,922.27	772,817.43	2,474,984.10	196,911.22	2,671,895.32	0.65	1.47	0.48	0.21	0.31	0.07
31/10/06	1,746,942.03	1,173,596.95	531,930.21	792,052.66	2,497,579.82	197,030.98	2,694,610.80	0.65	1.49	0.47	0.21	0.32	0.07
30/11/06	1,785,823.69	1,187,355.37	538,570.62	856,715.87	2,582,641.86	197,173.76	2,779,815.62	0.64	1.50	0.46	0.21	0.33	0.07
31/12/06	1,804,754.68	1,233,660.04	544,743.72	819,469.14	2,597,872.90	195,371.78	2,793,244.68	0.65	1.46	0.47	0.21	0.32	0.07
31/01/07	1,811,502.50	1,204,948.29	547,169.35	850,362.63	2,602,480.27	196,864.88	2,799,345.15	0.65	1.50	0.46	0.21	0.33	0.07
28/02/07	1,815,507.10	1,205,506.85	560,366.91	853,817.58	2,619,691.34	197,959.88	2,817,651.22	0.64	1.51	0.46	0.21	0.33	0.07

(continued)

Table A1 (continued)

Date	Loans to residents	Deposits of residents	Bonds issued	Other liabilities	Total Liabilities (Deposits + Bonds + Others)	Equity	Total liabilities and equity = Total assets	Loans to Total Assets	Loans to Deposits	Deposits over liabilities	Bonds over liabilities	Other liabilities over liabilities	Equity over Total Assets
31/03/07	1,840,808.32	1,235,851.36	566,362.32	860,444.94	2,662,658.62	230,085.74	2,892,744.36	0.64	1.49	0.46	0.21	0.32	0.08
30/04/07	1,843,496.36	1,230,190.22	570,832.19	899,259.90	2,700,282.31	238,387.39	2,938,669.70	0.63	1.50	0.46	0.21	0.33	0.08
31/05/07	1,864,268.84	1,254,219.66	578,823.95	926,864.61	2,759,908.22	235,398.44	2,995,306.66	0.62	1.49	0.45	0.21	0.34	0.08
30/06/07	1,890,620.87	1,257,932.81	581,731.62	942,285.10	2,781,949.53	235,859.48	3,017,809.01	0.63	1.50	0.45	0.21	0.34	0.08
31/07/07	1,903,948.99	1,257,294.95	582,697.40	952,480.22	2,792,472.57	241,633.78	3,034,106.35	0.63	1.51	0.45	0.21	0.34	0.08
31/08/07	1,904,738.64	1,241,848.35	585,466.85	938,195.95	2,765,511.15	241,562.68	3,007,073.83	0.63	1.53	0.45	0.21	0.34	0.08
30/09/07	1,919,969.54	1,259,262.67	583,724.97	948,277.38	2,791,265.02	242,245.15	3,033,510.17	0.63	1.52	0.45	0.21	0.34	0.08
31/10/07	2,104,945.55	1,419,915.04	604,025.61	1,019,845.46	3,043,786.11	258,435.13	3,302,221.24	0.64	1.48	0.47	0.20	0.34	0.08
30/11/07	2,131,029.08	1,414,266.26	608,516.98	1,043,318.79	3,066,102.03	259,077.46	3,325,179.49	0.64	1.51	0.46	0.20	0.34	0.08
31/12/07	2,160,574.21	1,470,847.02	618,054.15	978,248.22	3,067,149.39	264,678.91	3,331,828.30	0.65	1.47	0.48	0.20	0.34	0.08
31/01/08	2,140,969.47	1,447,580.36	628,340.08	997,293.08	3,073,213.52	265,927.12	3,339,140.64	0.64	1.48	0.47	0.20	0.32	0.08
29/02/08	2,172,041.47	1,465,972.19	649,368.72	986,255.43	3,101,596.34	266,457.01	3,368,053.35	0.64	1.48	0.47	0.20	0.32	0.08
31/03/08	2,180,163.52	1,469,242.93	657,984.06	987,612.48	3,114,839.47	272,810.06	3,387,649.53	0.64	1.48	0.47	0.21	0.32	0.08
30/04/08	2,178,635.93	1,491,208.88	669,372.03	990,668.67	3,151,249.58	272,414.61	3,423,664.19	0.64	1.46	0.47	0.21	0.32	0.08
31/05/08	2,223,331.31	1,548,993.96	687,709.62	1,013,510.01	3,250,213.59	278,429.16	3,528,642.75	0.63	1.44	0.48	0.21	0.31	0.08
30/06/08	2,229,257.11	1,520,282.66	702,953.40	1,015,742.89	3,238,978.95	278,436.84	3,517,415.79	0.63	1.47	0.47	0.21	0.31	0.08
31/07/08	2,232,961.01	1,514,367.58	707,212.65	999,669.63	3,221,249.86	278,315.29	3,499,565.15	0.64	1.47	0.47	0.22	0.31	0.08
31/08/08	2,239,887.17	1,519,187.44	709,892.41	997,325.09	3,226,404.94	278,813.22	3,505,218.16	0.64	1.47	0.47	0.22	0.31	0.08
30/09/08	2,266,571.13	1,550,425.16	717,944.48	1,018,159.75	3,286,529.39	277,765.17	3,564,294.56	0.64	1.46	0.47	0.22	0.31	0.08
31/10/08	2,496,898.55	1,806,405.59	733,444.56	1,000,783.68	3,540,633.83	278,021.73	3,818,655.56	0.65	1.38	0.51	0.21	0.28	0.07
30/11/08	2,347,471.03	1,669,103.80	740,191.90	1,030,060.17	3,439,355.87	275,868.44	3,715,224.31	0.63	1.41	0.49	0.22	0.30	0.07
31/12/08	2,322,468.76	1,656,857.90	740,520.55	960,758.97	3,358,137.42	276,426.86	3,634,564.28	0.64	1.40	0.49	0.22	0.29	0.08
31/01/09	2,335,363.21	1,649,875.08	745,532.44	963,771.46	3,359,178.98	276,296.22	3,635,475.20	0.64	1.42	0.49	0.22	0.29	0.08
28/02/09	2,347,433.02	1,646,327.12	767,629.56	960,815.86	3,374,772.54	279,750.58	3,654,523.12	0.64	1.43	0.49	0.23	0.28	0.08
31/03/09	2,344,941.48	1,664,123.86	788,018.54	977,055.32	3,429,197.72	279,611.55	3,708,809.27	0.63	1.41	0.49	0.23	0.28	0.08
30/04/09	2,327,400.65	1,657,275.92	799,401.63	947,000.33	3,403,677.88	287,670.88	3,691,348.76	0.63	1.40	0.49	0.23	0.28	0.08
31/05/09	2,331,906.23	1,660,736.34	804,493.56	931,586.07	3,396,815.97	288,318.62	3,685,134.59	0.63	1.40	0.49	0.24	0.27	0.08
30/06/09	2,348,556.27	1,671,512.52	808,490.05	924,420.48	3,404,423.05	289,417.83	3,693,840.88	0.64	1.41	0.49	0.24	0.27	0.08
31/07/09	2,324,873.12	1,659,704.29	812,123.98	919,322.88	3,391,151.15	290,970.52	3,682,121.67	0.63	1.40	0.49	0.24	0.27	0.08
31/08/09	2,310,341.93	1,650,616.75	814,406.71	896,667.30	3,361,690.76	291,029.45	3,652,720.21	0.63	1.40	0.49	0.24	0.27	0.08
30/09/09	2,323,550.75	1,669,509.75	815,744.40	893,333.37	3,378,587.52	292,094.18	3,670,681.70	0.63	1.39	0.49	0.24	0.26	0.08
31/10/09	2,327,652.75	1,688,212.92	811,687.85	880,153.10	3,380,053.87	290,656.48	3,670,710.35	0.63	1.38	0.50	0.24	0.26	0.08
30/11/09	2,361,636.08	1,700,761.71	815,811.34	913,580.63	3,430,153.68	291,753.62	3,721,907.30	0.63	1.39	0.50	0.24	0.27	0.08

(continued)

Table A1 (continued)

Date	Loans to residents	Deposits of residents	Bonds issued	Other liabilities	Total Liabilities (Deposits + Bonds + Others)	Equity	Total liabilities and equity = Total assets	Loans to Total Assets	Loans to Deposits	Deposits over liabilities	Bonds over liabili-ties	Other liabilities over liabilities	Equity over Total Assets
31/12/09	2,374,453.68	1,732,498.88	819,600.70	844,656.78	3,396,756.36	293,935.99	3,690,692.35	0.64	1.37	0.51	0.24	0.25	0.08
31/01/10	2,357,249.82	1,728,180.49	820,718.58	861,795.92	3,410,694.99	298,453.70	3,709,148.69	0.64	1.36	0.51	0.24	0.25	0.08
28/02/10	2,354,176.83	1,723,596.00	815,076.43	881,262.28	3,419,934.71	298,559.28	3,718,493.99	0.63	1.37	0.50	0.24	0.26	0.08
31/03/10	2,352,358.71	1,720,582.73	815,560.39	880,520.65	3,416,663.77	299,057.40	3,715,721.17	0.63	1.37	0.50	0.24	0.26	0.08
30/04/10	2,353,988.69	1,734,036.98	814,030.31	891,562.77	3,439,630.06	302,062.21	3,741,692.27	0.63	1.36	0.50	0.24	0.26	0.08
31/05/10	2,365,973.56	1,770,143.19	812,850.47	934,462.03	3,517,455.69	302,850.55	3,820,306.24	0.62	1.34	0.50	0.23	0.27	0.08
30/06/10	2,438,980.70	1,931,227.81	806,870.12	845,880.57	3,583,978.50	359,999.16	3,943,977.66	0.62	1.26	0.54	0.23	0.24	0.09
31/07/10	2,425,118.28	1,920,330.78	807,719.33	831,967.27	3,560,017.38	360,533.65	3,920,551.03	0.62	1.26	0.54	0.23	0.23	0.09
31/08/10	2,422,752.50	1,888,922.15	811,148.24	895,840.83	3,595,911.22	360,868.84	3,956,780.06	0.61	1.28	0.53	0.23	0.25	0.09
30/09/10	2,447,334.75	1,897,778.19	815,103.41	885,036.40	3,597,918.00	361,273.96	3,959,191.96	0.62	1.29	0.53	0.23	0.25	0.09
31/10/10	2,431,805.94	1,904,505.66	812,907.44	836,547.63	3,553,960.73	361,510.63	3,915,471.36	0.62	1.28	0.54	0.23	0.24	0.09
30/11/10	2,316,117.47	1,758,047.04	812,320.08	871,997.11	3,442,364.23	345,781.06	3,788,145.29	0.61	1.32	0.51	0.24	0.25	0.09
31/12/10	2,318,427.64	1,825,622.12	807,691.36	776,130.15	3,409,443.63	349,447.08	3,758,890.71	0.62	1.27	0.54	0.24	0.23	0.09
31/01/11	2,342,198.04	1,807,106.83	807,693.58	800,553.65	3,415,354.06	363,068.29	3,778,422.35	0.62	1.30	0.53	0.24	0.23	0.10
28/02/11	2,358,159.48	1,803,756.76	812,390.26	800,748.37	3,416,895.39	368,463.20	3,785,358.59	0.62	1.31	0.53	0.24	0.23	0.10
31/03/11	2,343,411.10	1,766,156.31	832,743.80	788,232.22	3,387,132.33	368,296.30	3,755,428.63	0.62	1.33	0.52	0.25	0.23	0.10
30/04/11	2,342,099.16	1,779,760.77	835,010.56	771,560.56	3,386,331.89	370,058.11	3,756,390.00	0.62	1.32	0.53	0.25	0.23	0.10
31/05/11	2,358,927.31	1,764,765.59	846,070.99	807,019.63	3,417,856.21	373,876.87	3,791,733.08	0.62	1.34	0.52	0.25	0.24	0.10
30/06/11	2,357,196.72	1,769,473.27	844,134.19	785,896.38	3,399,503.84	379,937.19	3,779,441.03	0.62	1.33	0.52	0.25	0.23	0.10
31/07/11	2,349,802.51	1,813,173.19	847,356.10	771,212.43	3,431,741.72	382,171.90	3,813,913.62	0.62	1.30	0.53	0.25	0.22	0.10
31/08/11	2,348,509.86	1,824,092.33	850,394.21	788,778.99	3,463,265.53	382,362.15	3,845,627.68	0.61	1.29	0.53	0.25	0.23	0.10
30/09/11	2,390,147.89	1,869,141.34	860,453.00	838,555.34	3,568,149.68	383,297.58	3,951,447.26	0.60	1.28	0.52	0.24	0.24	0.10
31/10/11	2,389,931.10	1,882,824.07	858,156.62	822,500.21	3,563,480.90	383,241.31	3,946,722.21	0.61	1.27	0.53	0.24	0.23	0.10
30/11/11	2,397,265.42	1,890,155.75	865,085.97	844,149.41	3,599,391.13	385,525.67	3,984,916.80	0.60	1.27	0.53	0.24	0.23	0.10
31/12/11	2,374,568.73	1,945,688.63	914,227.14	795,272.74	3,655,188.51	379,559.00	4,034,747.51	0.59	1.22	0.53	0.25	0.22	0.09
31/01/12	2,367,914.89	1,941,846.61	940,089.17	813,233.46	3,695,169.24	390,666.00	4,085,835.24	0.58	1.22	0.53	0.25	0.22	0.10
29/02/12	2,347,342.20	1,961,870.94	956,029.00	803,598.25	3,721,498.19	392,568.00	4,114,066.19	0.57	1.20	0.53	0.26	0.22	0.10
31/03/12	2,364,443.35	2,026,315.77	959,936.21	758,448.12	3,744,700.10	394,564.00	4,139,264.10	0.57	1.17	0.54	0.26	0.20	0.10
30/04/12	2,371,011.67	2,035,433.98	942,940.18	808,399.04	3,786,773.20	383,247.00	4,170,020.20	0.57	1.16	0.54	0.25	0.21	0.09
31/05/12	2,364,585.83	2,034,126.45	945,494.46	852,708.04	3,832,328.95	370,287.00	4,202,615.95	0.56	1.16	0.53	0.25	0.22	0.09
30/06/12	2,371,009.56	2,076,381.08	953,322.52	793,390.97	3,823,094.57	372,321.11	4,195,415.68	0.57	1.14	0.54	0.25	0.21	0.09
31/07/12	2,378,614.07	2,070,965.56	966,302.09	832,669.40	3,869,937.05	371,492.72	4,241,429.77	0.56	1.15	0.54	0.25	0.22	0.09
31/08/12	2,366,229.96	2,070,098.68	962,194.95	820,726.40	3,853,020.03	371,785.10	4,224,805.13	0.56	1.14	0.54	0.25	0.21	0.09

(continued)

Table A1 (continued)

Date	Loans to residents	Deposits of residents	Bonds issued	Other liabilities	Total Liabilities (Deposits + Bonds + Others)	Equity	Total liabilities and equity = Total assets	Loans to Total Assets	Loans to Deposits	Deposits over liabilities	Bonds over liabilities	Other liabilities over liabilities	Equity over Total Assets
30/09/12	2,399,185.09	2,112,032.59	961,827.17	794,805.60	3,868,665.36	370,794.51	4,239,459.87	0.57	1.14	0.55	0.25	0.21	0.09
31/10/12	2,377,039.80	2,075,503.35	961,643.54	815,714.21	3,852,861.10	371,523.09	4,224,384.19	0.56	1.15	0.54	0.25	0.21	0.09
30/11/12	2,391,402.46	2,074,580.52	957,594.38	843,814.77	3,875,989.67	371,054.84	4,247,044.51	0.56	1.15	0.54	0.25	0.21	0.09
31/12/12	2,356,373.20	2,079,347.30	958,332.49	800,427.93	3,838,107.72	372,907.01	4,211,014.73	0.56	1.13	0.54	0.25	0.22	0.09
31/01/13	2,353,419.19	2,065,186.26	960,055.34	777,820.08	3,803,061.68	380,003.47	4,183,065.15	0.56	1.14	0.54	0.25	0.21	0.09
28/02/13	2,377,063.14	2,107,194.01	948,596.48	772,389.19	3,828,179.68	385,537.13	4,213,716.81	0.56	1.13	0.55	0.25	0.20	0.09
31/03/13	2,354,169.16	2,130,196.72	928,879.09	765,861.67	3,824,937.48	388,025.30	4,212,962.78	0.56	1.11	0.56	0.25	0.20	0.09
30/04/13	2,355,885.42	2,139,580.88	913,736.96	790,255.96	3,843,573.80	382,179.36	4,225,753.16	0.56	1.10	0.56	0.24	0.20	0.09
31/05/13	2,343,088.26	2,129,811.54	912,740.89	771,411.21	3,813,963.64	382,319.05	4,196,282.69	0.56	1.10	0.56	0.24	0.21	0.09
30/06/13	2,319,191.26	2,131,020.91	913,512.60	734,649.61	3,779,183.12	381,892.94	4,161,076.06	0.56	1.09	0.56	0.24	0.20	0.09
31/07/13	2,304,650.32	2,094,837.43	905,003.65	747,737.21	3,747,578.29	382,690.55	4,130,268.84	0.56	1.10	0.56	0.24	0.19	0.09
31/08/13	2,300,744.50	2,111,587.86	899,813.68	711,482.17	3,722,883.71	383,615.45	4,106,499.16	0.56	1.09	0.56	0.24	0.20	0.09
30/09/13	2,310,439.65	2,105,413.93	892,078.06	732,932.71	3,730,424.70	386,084.33	4,116,509.03	0.56	1.10	0.57	0.24	0.19	0.09
31/10/13	2,304,172.96	2,093,913.25	893,560.07	740,961.89	3,728,435.21	386,560.26	4,114,995.47	0.56	1.10	0.56	0.24	0.20	0.09
30/11/13	2,307,524.19	2,106,620.81	886,884.06	717,332.05	3,710,836.92	387,528.22	4,098,365.14	0.56	1.10	0.56	0.24	0.20	0.09
31/12/13	2,288,649.67	2,082,486.58	878,351.73	686,816.80	3,647,655.11	390,651.54	4,038,306.65	0.57	1.10	0.57	0.24	0.19	0.09
31/01/14	2,309,625.83	2,075,458.77	871,451.36	717,904.10	3,664,814.23	399,693.61	4,064,507.84	0.57	1.11	0.57	0.24	0.19	0.10
28/02/14	2,311,488.45	2,091,500.04	861,623.10	695,720.88	3,648,844.02	405,353.65	4,054,197.67	0.57	1.11	0.57	0.24	0.20	0.10
31/03/14	2,322,964.81	2,108,667.04	830,006.13	695,844.31	3,634,517.48	420,996.57	4,055,514.05	0.57	1.10	0.57	0.24	0.19	0.10
30/04/14	2,293,798.65	2,085,246.16	825,388.35	694,105.43	3,604,739.94	423,070.64	4,027,810.58	0.57	1.10	0.58	0.23	0.19	0.10
31/05/14	2,275,446.04	2,081,311.88	813,616.35	695,941.23	3,590,869.46	404,628.63	3,995,498.09	0.57	1.09	0.58	0.23	0.19	0.11
30/06/14	2,307,081.35	2,087,310.80	802,135.14	720,483.60	3,609,929.54	411,000.46	4,020,930.00	0.57	1.11	0.58	0.23	0.19	0.10
31/07/14	2,305,074.25	2,085,281.69	783,566.23	716,087.55	3,584,935.47	414,959.55	3,999,895.02	0.58	1.11	0.58	0.22	0.20	0.10
31/08/14	2,284,918.04	2,097,610.22	772,270.00	706,480.25	3,576,360.47	416,013.38	3,992,373.85	0.57	1.09	0.59	0.22	0.20	0.10
30/09/14	2,297,161.77	2,096,992.23	765,817.05	725,899.06	3,588,708.34	419,845.83	4,008,554.17	0.57	1.10	0.58	0.21	0.20	0.10
31/10/14	2,280,885.38	2,104,132.46	738,614.67	722,900.93	3,565,648.06	419,492.10	3,985,140.16	0.57	1.08	0.59	0.21	0.20	0.10
30/11/14	2,307,385.53	2,132,743.71	734,064.04	731,010.47	3,597,818.22	418,102.47	4,015,920.69	0.57	1.08	0.59	0.20	0.20	0.11
31/12/14	2,313,837.57	2,136,720.77	727,136.55	726,256.89	3,590,114.21	424,235.15	4,014,349.36	0.58	1.08	0.60	0.20	0.20	0.10
31/01/15	2,314,733.48	2,151,179.89	718,589.57	762,609.77	3,632,379.23	436,371.77	4,068,751.00	0.57	1.08	0.59	0.20	0.20	0.11
28/02/15	2,307,289.81	2,152,334.79	698,641.11	759,058.90	3,610,034.80	438,270.12	4,048,304.92	0.57	1.07	0.60	0.19	0.21	0.11
31/03/15	2,332,899.46	2,175,396.72	687,426.96	773,929.08	3,636,752.76	438,045.59	4,074,798.35	0.57	1.07	0.60	0.19	0.21	0.11
30/04/15	2,320,459.82	2,159,792.53	677,489.44	770,117.91	3,607,399.88	424,250.57	4,031,650.45	0.58	1.07	0.60	0.19	0.21	0.11
31/05/15	2,317,822.94	2,172,413.32	668,742.14	748,128.83	3,589,284.29	426,402.15	4,015,686.44	0.58	1.07	0.61	0.19	0.21	0.11

(continued)

Table A1 (continued)

Date	Loans to residents	Deposits of residents	Bonds issued	Other liabilities	Total Liabilities (Deposits + Bonds + Others)	Equity	Total liabilities and equity = Total assets	Loans to Total Assets	Loans to Deposits	Deposits over liabilities	Bonds over liabilities	Other liabilities over liabilities	Equity over Total Assets
30/06/15	2,339,205.23	2,176,338.26	656,979.14	702,521.65	3,535,839.05	441,842.47	3,977,681.52	0.59	1.07	0.62	0.19	0.20	0.11
31/07/15	2,327,433.28	2,158,857.34	646,322.13	718,512.09	3,523,691.56	443,048.87	3,966,740.43	0.59	1.08	0.61	0.18	0.20	0.11
31/08/15	2,318,669.44	2,165,629.90	638,967.68	697,357.62	3,501,955.20	443,074.69	3,945,029.89	0.59	1.07	0.62	0.18	0.20	0.11
30/09/15	2,327,975.16	2,173,977.56	630,536.97	688,611.20	3,493,125.73	446,001.52	3,939,127.25	0.59	1.07	0.62	0.18	0.20	0.11
31/10/15	2,321,984.38	2,175,838.45	620,188.41	692,222.16	3,488,249.02	447,020.26	3,935,269.28	0.59	1.07	0.62	0.18	0.20	0.11
30/11/15	2,336,226.17	2,153,085.68	622,949.51	736,710.02	3,512,745.21	449,757.51	3,962,502.72	0.59	1.09	0.61	0.18	0.21	0.11
31/12/15	2,333,294.64	2,168,667.23	621,823.38	674,747.24	3,465,237.85	448,232.39	3,913,470.24	0.60	1.08	0.63	0.18	0.19	0.11
31/01/16	2,345,208.32	2,188,941.68	604,017.73	693,670.05	3,486,629.46	451,283.30	3,937,912.76	0.60	1.07	0.63	0.17	0.20	0.11
29/02/16	2,355,244.32	2,216,503.93	595,429.73	717,902.46	3,529,836.12	447,799.25	3,977,635.37	0.59	1.06	0.63	0.17	0.20	0.11
31/03/16	2,354,023.89	2,223,523.36	585,658.03	700,948.72	3,510,130.11	443,110.74	3,953,240.85	0.60	1.06	0.63	0.17	0.20	0.11
30/04/16	2,343,047.88	2,239,546.19	578,865.80	681,980.99	3,500,392.98	438,922.05	3,939,315.03	0.59	1.05	0.64	0.17	0.19	0.11
31/05/16	2,327,018.97	2,207,614.45	573,289.56	708,419.34	3,489,323.35	442,000.80	3,931,324.15	0.59	1.05	0.63	0.16	0.20	0.11
30/06/16	2,341,794.83	2,243,617.66	582,565.25	711,758.85	3,537,941.76	440,536.54	3,978,478.30	0.59	1.04	0.63	0.16	0.20	0.11
31/07/16	2,318,812.30	2,234,557.24	580,803.06	686,562.57	3,501,922.87	441,461.74	3,943,384.61	0.59	1.04	0.64	0.17	0.20	0.11
31/08/16	2,321,543.23	2,224,472.26	574,665.70	679,966.48	3,479,104.44	441,923.52	3,921,027.96	0.59	1.04	0.64	0.17	0.20	0.11
30/09/16	2,334,851.39	2,232,350.34	569,615.85	686,570.41	3,488,536.60	441,495.48	3,930,032.08	0.59	1.05	0.64	0.16	0.20	0.11
31/10/16	2,328,139.27	2,229,305.46	567,269.20	678,896.51	3,475,471.17	444,068.15	3,919,539.32	0.59	1.04	0.64	0.16	0.20	0.11
30/11/16	2,324,187.81	2,221,173.17	564,544.68	690,659.71	3,476,377.56	442,866.76	3,919,244.32	0.59	1.05	0.64	0.16	0.20	0.11
31/12/16	2,342,116.33	2,278,447.74	558,028.46	642,226.55	3,478,702.75	440,953.26	3,919,656.01	0.60	1.03	0.65	0.16	0.18	0.11
31/01/17	2,314,595.92	2,253,600.85	554,077.24	636,104.83	3,443,782.92	449,924.84	3,893,707.76	0.59	1.03	0.65	0.16	0.18	0.12
28/02/17	2,303,179.48	2,233,970.60	553,427.33	646,547.13	3,433,945.06	461,563.11	3,895,508.17	0.59	1.03	0.65	0.16	0.19	0.12
31/03/17	2,376,564.98	2,341,232.96	541,057.61	633,661.84	3,515,952.41	459,550.54	3,975,502.95	0.60	1.02	0.67	0.15	0.18	0.12
30/04/17	2,383,519.55	2,361,059.39	533,279.78	618,188.15	3,512,527.32	444,824.13	3,957,351.45	0.60	1.01	0.67	0.15	0.18	0.11
31/05/17	2,360,829.94	2,308,756.48	529,374.67	628,808.95	3,466,940.10	451,021.79	3,917,961.89	0.60	1.02	0.67	0.15	0.18	0.12
30/06/17	2,387,480.56	2,304,018.99	524,873.05	633,816.86	3,462,708.90	442,163.26	3,904,872.16	0.61	1.04	0.67	0.15	0.18	0.11

Table A2 Sampled banks listed according to the number of bond issuances; data gathered from "eXact 4 Suite"

	Listing		Seniority		Return					Total		
	Listed	Unlisted	Senior	Subordinated	Fixed rate	Fixed rate + variable	Fixed rate + Zero Coupon	Variable rate	Zero Coupon	Freq.	%	Cumul. (%)
Banco BPM	24	366	379	11	103	45	0	225	17	390	4.26	4.26
UBI Banca	22	354	359	17	250	68	0	45	13	376	4.10	8.36
Intesa SanPaolo	148	166	286	28	104	65	2	134	9	314	3.43	11.79
Banca Nazionale del Lavoro	105	165	270	0	115	38	0	106	11	270	2.95	14.74
Unicredit Group	106	146	203	49	89	53	0	96	14	252	2.75	17.49
Cassa Risparmio Asti	0	163	145	18	97	9	0	54	3	163	1.78	19.27
Banca IMI	130	21	151	0	58	60	2	25	6	151	1.65	20.92
Banca Monte dei Paschi di Siena	82	53	123	12	58	17	2	44	14	135	1.47	22.39
Banca Popolare di Sondrio	8	125	127	6	112	2	0	18	1	133	1.45	23.84
BCC CRAS Toscano - Siena	112	13	125	0	55	49	0	16	5	125	1.36	25.21
MedioBanca	99	20	113	6	30	57	0	25	7	119	1.30	26.51
Banca Popolare Emilia Romagna	5	103	99	9	72	4	0	21	11	108	1.18	27.69
Banca Tema Maremma Pitigliano	96	11	104	3	84	11	0	4	8	107	1.17	28.85
Banca Popolare Pugliese	0	103	103	0	62	30	0	11	0	103	1.12	29.98
Cassa Risparmio San Miniato	60	25	76	9	73	2	0	2	8	85	0.93	30.91
Credito Valtellinese	48	32	76	4	60	3	0	16	1	80	0.87	31.78
Unipol Gruppo Finanziario	2	77	75	4	72	0	0	5	2	79	0.86	32.64
BCC Alba Langhe e Roero	0	76	75	1	68	0	0	7	1	76	0.83	33.47
Banca Carige Italia	6	67	68	5	30	11	0	32	0	73	0.80	34.27
Banco di Desio	61	12	68	5	61	4	0	8	0	73	0.80	35.07
Cassa Risparmio Biella Vercelli	0	72	72	0	52	6	0	13	1	72	0.79	35.85
Banca Popolare di Vicenza	46	25	65	6	57	4	0	4	6	71	0.78	36.63
Cassa Risparmio Ravenna	14	57	56	15	54	6	0	6	5	71	0.78	37.40
BCC Sant'Elena	0	67	67	0	66	0	0	1	0	67	0.73	38.13

(continued)

Table A2 (continued)

	Listing		Seniority		Return					Total		
	Listed	Unlisted	Senior	Subordinated	Fixed rate	Fixed rate + variable	Fixed rate + Zero Coupon	Variable rate	Zero Coupon	Freq.	%	Cumul. (%)
Banca Sella	0	62	13	49	51	0	0	11	0	62	0.68	38.81
BCC Ravennate e Imolese	46	14	60	0	42	5	0	13	0	60	0.66	39.47
Banca Popolare Etica	0	59	42	17	48	8	0	3	0	59	0.64	40.11
Banca Popolare Alto Adige	0	58	58	0	26	2	0	29	1	58	0.63	40.74
BCC Centroveneto	0	56	51	5	45	3	0	4	4	56	0.61	41.35
Veneto Banca	17	39	47	9	36	8	0	9	3	56	0.61	41.97
CRU Alto Adige	0	55	55	0	32	1	0	22	0	55	0.60	42.57
BCC Chianti Fiorentino	44	7	50	1	33	9	0	0	9	51	0.56	43.12
Banca Popolare Sant'Angelo	0	51	47	4	50	0	0	0	1	51	0.56	43.68
BCC Alta Toscana Vignole/ Masiano	47	3	50	0	26	0	0	24	0	50	0.55	44.22
Banca di Imola	10	40	40	10	45	2	0	2	1	50	0.55	44.77
Cassa Risparmio Rimini	0	50	40	10	23	8	0	18	1	50	0.55	45.32
BCC Cassa Padana	0	48	48	0	44	0	0	0	4	48	0.52	45.84
BCC Roma	5	42	47	0	39	6	0	2	0	47	0.51	46.35
BCC di Pescia e Cascina	37	10	46	1	46	1	0	0	0	47	0.51	46.87
BCC Bologna	0	46	46	0	26	9	0	9	2	46	0.50	47.37
BCC Fornacette	0	46	42	4	45	1	0	0	0	46	0.50	47.87
BCC Caravaggio Adda e Cremasco	0	45	45	0	42	0	0	3	0	45	0.49	48.36
Banca Popolare S.Felice Panaro	0	45	45	0	41	0	0	4	0	45	0.49	48.85
BCC del Territorio Lombardo	0	44	41	3	42	0	0	2	0	44	0.48	49.33
Banca Popolare di Bergamo CV	0	44	44	0	40	0	0	3	1	44	0.48	49.81
Cassa Risparmio Volterra	0	44	42	2	44	0	0	0	0	44	0.48	50.29
BCC Pianfei e Rocca De' Baldi	0	43	43	0	38	4	0	1	0	43	0.47	50.76

(continued)

Table A2 (continued)

	Listing		Seniority		Return					Total		
	Listed	Unlisted	Senior	Subordinated	Fixed rate	Fixed rate + variable	Fixed rate + Zero Coupon	Variable rate	Zero Coupon	Freq.	%	Cumul. (%)
BCC Laudense	15	27	37	5	40	0	0	0	2	42	0.46	51.22
Cassa Risparmio Bolzano	0	42	40	2	15	2	0	24	1	42	0.46	51.68
BCC dell'Oglio e del Serio	0	41	35	6	32	7	0	2	0	41	0.45	52.13
ICCREA	33	8	38	3	22	15	0	4	0	41	0.45	52.58
Banca Agricola Popolare Ragusa	0	40	40	0	40	0	0	0	0	40	0.44	53.01
Iccrea BancaImpresa	0	40	40	0	23	0	0	17	0	40	0.44	53.45
BCC Bergamo e Valli	0	39	32	7	33	6	0	0	0	39	0.43	53.88
BCC Casalgrasso e Sant'Albano	0	39	39	0	14	8	0	17	0	39	0.43	54.30
BCC Valdinievole	29	9	36	2	27	3	0	7	1	38	0.41	54.72
Banca Valsabbina	1	37	33	5	37	0	0	1	0	38	0.41	55.13
CRU Adamello Brenta	0	38	37	1	26	7	0	2	3	38	0.41	55.55
Cassa Risparmio Bra	2	36	33	5	25	3	0	8	2	38	0.41	55.96
Nuova Banca delle Marche	0	38	38	0	25	0	0	0	13	38	0.41	56.38
BCC Popolare	17	20	37	0	37	0	0	0	0	37	0.40	56.78
BCC Bergamasca e Orobica	0	36	36	0	32	0	0	1	3	36	0.39	57.17
BCC Emil	0	36	34	2	29	6	0	1	0	36	0.39	57.57
BCC Treviglio e Geradadda	0	36	31	5	26	5	0	3	2	36	0.39	57.96
BCC Friuli Centrale	0	35	35	0	32	2	0	0	1	35	0.38	58.34
Banco di Sardegna	0	35	35	0	31	0	0	4	0	35	0.38	58.72
CRA Cantu'	0	35	35	0	19	4	0	11	1	35	0.38	59.10
Cassa Risparmio Cesena	28	7	28	7	23	3	0	8	1	35	0.38	59.49
BCC Friuli (Credifriuli)	34	0	34	0	25	2	0	7	0	34	0.37	59.86
Credito Emiliano	7	27	29	5	17	12	0	5	0	34	0.37	60.23
BCC Carate Brianza	0	33	33	0	21	2	0	8	2	33	0.36	60.59
BCC Centropadana	0	33	33	0	23	3	0	2	5	33	0.36	60.95
BCC Cremasca e Mantovana	0	33	32	1	31	0	0	2	0	33	0.36	61.31
BCC G. Toniolo di San Cataldo	8	25	31	2	30	0	0	2	1	33	0.36	61.67
Credito Siciliano	22	10	30	2	29	0	0	3	0	32	0.35	62.02
BCC Picena Truentina	0	31	31	0	22	9	0	0	0	31	0.34	62.36

(continued)

Table A2 (continued)

	Listing		Seniority		Return					Total		
	Listed	Unlisted	Senior	Subordinated	Fixed rate	Fixed rate + variable	Fixed rate + Zero Coupon	Variable rate	Zero Coupon	Freq.	%	Cumul. (%)
BCC Signa	30	1	31	0	26	5	0	0	0	31	0.34	62.70
CRA Binasco BCC	0	31	31	0	31	0	0	0	0	31	0.34	63.03
CRA Brendola	0	31	30	1	24	0	0	5	2	31	0.34	63.37
BCC Cambiano	0	30	30	0	26	0	0	3	1	30	0.33	63.70
BCC Udine	0	30	29	1	23	2	0	5	0	30	0.33	64.03
BCC Verona-Cadidavid	0	30	30	0	25	2	0	2	1	30	0.33	64.36
CR Pergine	0	30	30	0	7	4	0	17	2	30	0.33	64.68
Friulovest Banca	0	30	30	0	26	0	0	0	4	30	0.33	65.01
BCC Alpi Marittime Carru'	0	29	26	3	24	2	0	1	2	29	0.32	65.33
Cassa Risparmio Cento	0	29	27	2	22	0	0	5	2	29	0.32	65.64
BCC Cherasco	0	28	26	2	24	0	0	4	0	28	0.31	65.95
BCC Valdostana	0	28	22	6	23	4	0	1	0	28	0.31	66.26
Banca Nuova	19	9	27	1	20	1	0	0	7	28	0.31	66.56
Banca Valdarno	22	6	25	3	20	6	0	2	0	28	0.31	66.87
BCC Triuggio	0	27	27	0	27	0	0	0	0	27	0.29	67.16
Cassa Risparmio Savigliano	2	25	24	3	24	0	0	3	0	27	0.29	67.46
BCC Giudicarie Paganella	0	26	22	4	22	0	0	2	2	26	0.28	67.74
BCC Manzano	0	26	26	0	18	4	0	4	0	26	0.28	68.02
BCC Pistoia	18	8	22	4	14	0	0	7	5	26	0.28	68.31
CRA Val di Fassa e Agordino	0	26	26	0	17	0	0	3	6	26	0.28	68.59
CRU Tuenno Val di Non	0	26	26	0	18	0	0	7	1	26	0.28	68.88
Nuova Banca Etruria e Lazio	0	26	26	0	26	0	0	0	0	26	0.28	69.16
BCC Caraglio e Riviera dei Fiori	0	25	25	0	18	6	0	1	0	25	0.27	69.43
BCC Centro Emilia (Cento Crev.)	0	25	25	0	23	1	0	1	0	25	0.27	69.71
BCC Impruneta	25	0	25	0	19	3	0	1	2	25	0.27	69.98
BCC Metauro	0	25	25	0	19	1	0	0	5	25	0.27	70.25
BCC Montepulciano	25	0	25	0	25	0	0	0	0	25	0.27	70.52

(continued)

Table A2 (continued)

	Listing		Seniority		Return					Total		
	Listed	Unlisted	Senior	Subordinated	Fixed rate	Fixed rate + variable	Fixed rate + Zero Coupon	Variable rate	Zero Coupon	Freq.	%	Cumul. (%)
BCC Vicentino Pojana Maggiore	0	25	23	2	22	0	0	3	0	25	0.27	70.80
Banca Popolare di Spoleto	4	21	23	2	18	1	0	4	2	25	0.27	71.07
BCC Brescia	24	0	24	0	24	0	0	0	0	24	0.26	71.33
BCC Crediveneto	20	4	21	3	23	0	0	0	1	24	0.26	71.59
BCC Forli'	6	18	19	5	16	1	0	1	6	24	0.26	71.86
Cassa Risparmio Chieti	0	24	24	0	22	0	0	0	2	24	0.26	72.12
Cassa Risparmio Fossano	0	24	22	2	24	0	0	0	0	24	0.26	72.38
BCC Basso Sebino	0	23	23	0	8	15	0	0	0	23	0.25	72.63
BCC Carugate e Inzago	21	2	23	0	21	2	0	0	0	23	0.25	72.88
BCC Pontassieve	17	6	23	0	19	0	0	4	0	23	0.25	73.13
BCC Versilia LunigianaGarfagnana	20	3	23	0	22	1	0	0	0	23	0.25	73.38
Sviluppo della Coop. di Credito	21	2	21	2	21	0	0	2	0	23	0.25	73.64
BCC Alto Vicentino	0	22	21	1	14	0	0	5	3	22	0.24	73.88
BCC Area Pratese	18	4	22	0	13	8	0	0	1	22	0.24	74.12
BCC Castagneto Carducci	0	22	22	0	20	2	0	0	0	22	0.24	74.36
BCC Colli Morenici del Garda	0	22	15	7	21	0	0	1	0	22	0.24	74.60
BCC Fiumicello ed Aiello	0	22	22	0	19	2	0	1	0	22	0.24	74.84
BCC Marcon	0	22	20	2	14	1	0	7	0	22	0.24	75.08
BCC S.Giorgio Quinto Valle Agno	0	22	15	7	12	4	0	3	3	22	0.24	75.32
BancApulia	0	22	21	1	17	4	0	0	1	22	0.24	75.56
Banca Popolare Comm. e Ind.	0	22	22	0	16	1	0	3	2	22	0.24	75.80
BCC Piove di Sacco	0	21	20	1	21	0	0	0	0	21	0.23	76.03
BCC Prealpi	0	21	21	0	21	0	0	0	0	21	0.23	76.26

(continued)

Table A2 (continued)

	Listing		Seniority		Return					Total		
	Listed	Unlisted	Senior	Subordinated	Fixed rate	Fixed rate + variable	Fixed rate + Zero Coupon	Variable rate	Zero Coupon	Freq.	%	Cumul. (%)
BCC Rimini	0	21	21	0	17	4	0	0	0	21	0.23	76.48
BCC San Biagio	0	21	21	0	14	5	0	2	0	21	0.23	76.71
BCC Valdichiana Tosco Umbro	20	1	21	0	21	0	0	0	0	21	0.23	76.94
BCC Veronese di Concamarise	0	21	21	0	19	1	0	1	0	21	0.23	77.17
CRU Merano	0	21	21	0	6	1	0	13	1	21	0.23	77.40
CRU Mezzocorona	0	21	21	0	13	0	0	2	6	21	0.23	77.63
Cassa Risparmio Ferrara	0	21	21	0	16	0	0	1	4	21	0.23	77.86
Rovigo Banca	0	21	14	7	19	0	0	2	0	21	0.23	78.09
BCC Staranzano e Villesse	0	20	20	0	16	2	0	2	0	20	0.22	78.31
Banca Mediolanum	0	20	15	5	3	0	0	2	15	20	0.22	78.53
VIBanca	14	6	18	2	4	0	0	16	0	20	0.22	78.74
BCC Bene Vagienna	0	19	18	1	15	4	0	0	0	19	0.21	78.95
BCC Castel Goffredo	0	19	11	8	18	1	0	0	0	19	0.21	79.16
BCC Centromarca	0	19	19	0	17	0	0	2	0	19	0.21	79.37
BCC Lucinico Farra e Capriva	0	19	19	0	10	1	0	5	3	19	0.21	79.57
BCC Pachino	16	3	19	0	19	0	0	0	0	19	0.21	79.78
BCC Romagna Occidentale	0	19	19	0	12	1	0	6	0	19	0.21	79.99
CRA Boves	0	19	19	0	17	2	0	0	0	19	0.21	80.20
CRU Lavis	0	19	19	0	17	0	0	0	2	19	0.21	80.40
BCC Crediumbria	18	0	18	0	18	0	0	0	0	18	0.20	80.60
BCC Fano	0	18	17	1	17	0	0	0	1	18	0.20	80.80
BCC Agro Bresciano	0	17	12	5	17	0	0	0	0	17	0.19	80.98
BCC Castenaso	0	17	17	0	14	1	0	2	0	17	0.19	81.17
BCC Pordenonese	0	17	17	0	17	0	0	0	0	17	0.19	81.35
BCC Sala di Cesenatico	0	17	16	1	4	9	0	4	0	17	0.19	81.54
Banca di Sassari	0	17	17	0	15	0	0	2	0	17	0.19	81.72
CR Mori-Brentonico Val di Gresta	0	17	17	0	12	0	0	3	2	17	0.19	81.91
CR Val di Sole	0	17	17	0	11	2	0	3	1	17	0.19	82.10
CRU Valli di Primiero e Vanoi	0	17	16	1	8	0	0	7	2	17	0.19	82.28

(continued)

Table A2 (continued)

	Listing		Seniority		Return					Total		
	Listed	Unlisted	Senior	Subordinated	Fixed rate	Fixed rate + variable	Fixed rate + Zero Coupon	Variable rate	Zero Coupon	Freq.	%	Cumul. (%)
BCC Alta Brianza	0	16	16	0	9	0	0	6	1	16	0.17	82.46
BCC Mediocrati	10	6	11	5	16	0	0	0	0	16	0.17	82.63
BCC Monastier e del Sile	0	16	15	1	15	0	0	1	0	16	0.17	82.81
BCC Ostra e Morro d'Alba	0	16	16	0	14	0	0	0	2	16	0.17	82.98
BCC Romagna Est	0	16	16	0	11	5	0	0	0	16	0.17	83.16
Banca di Piacenza	0	16	16	0	15	0	0	1	0	16	0.17	83.33
CRA Cortina d'Ampezzo	0	16	16	0	5	5	0	6	0	16	0.17	83.50
BCC Basiliano	0	15	15	0	10	2	0	3	0	15	0.16	83.67
BCC Cernusco sul Naviglio	14	1	13	2	14	0	0	1	0	15	0.16	83.83
BCC Crotonese	13	2	11	4	15	0	0	0	0	15	0.16	84.00
BCC Marca	0	15	15	0	14	0	0	1	0	15	0.16	84.16
BCC Monte Pruno di Roscigno	0	15	15	0	15	0	0	0	0	15	0.16	84.32
BCC Picena	0	15	15	0	10	0	0	5	0	15	0.16	84.49
BCC Romano e Santa Caterina	0	15	13	2	11	2	0	2	0	15	0.16	84.65
Banca Popolare del Lazio	0	15	15	0	15	0	0	0	0	15	0.16	84.81
Banca Popolare di Cividale	4	11	13	2	5	8	0	2	0	15	0.16	84.98
Banca del Piemonte	0	15	15	0	8	6	0	1	0	15	0.16	85.14
Cassa Raiffeisen di Prato-Tubre	0	15	15	0	6	0	0	9	0	15	0.16	85.31
Credito Padano Banca Credito Cooperti..	0	15	13	2	14	0	0	0	1	15	0.16	85.47
BCC Ancona	0	14	11	3	9	0	0	3	2	14	0.15	85.62
BCC Anghiari e Stia	12	2	12	2	11	0	0	2	1	14	0.15	85.78
BCC Fiemme	0	14	14	0	9	0	0	2	3	14	0.15	85.93
BCC Pergola	0	14	14	0	14	0	0	0	0	14	0.15	86.08
BCC Rovereto	0	14	9	5	10	2	0	0	2	14	0.15	86.23
Banco Paolo Azzoaglio	0	14	13	1	11	0	0	3	0	14	0.15	86.39
Cassa Risparmio Saluzzo	0	14	12	2	13	0	0	1	0	14	0.15	86.54
BCC Aldeno e Cadine	0	13	13	0	10	0	0	1	2	13	0.14	86.68
BCC Arborea	7	6	13	0	13	0	0	0	0	13	0.14	86.82

(continued)

Table A2 (continued)

	Listing		Seniority		Return					Total		
	Listed	Unlisted	Senior	Subordinated	Fixed rate	Fixed rate + variable	Fixed rate + Zero Coupon	Variable rate	Zero Coupon	Freq.	%	Cumul. (%)
BCC Busto Garolfo e Buguggiate	0	13	13	0	12	1	0	0	0	13	0.14	86.97
BCC Colli Euganei	0	13	12	1	12	0	0	1	0	13	0.14	87.11
BCC Filottrano	0	13	13	0	10	0	0	0	3	13	0.14	87.25
BCC Malatestiana	0	13	13	0	8	5	0	0	0	13	0.14	87.39
Banca Popolare Puglia Basilicata	0	13	8	5	13	0	0	0	0	13	0.14	87.53
Banca Popolare di Bari	0	13	7	6	10	1	0	0	2	13	0.14	87.67
CRA Bolzano	0	13	13	0	2	0	0	11	0	13	0.14	87.82
CRU Alto Garda	0	13	13	0	10	0	0	1	2	13	0.14	87.96
CRU Novella e Alta Anaunia	0	13	13	0	9	0	0	2	2	13	0.14	88.10
BCC Atestina	0	12	12	0	11	0	0	1	0	12	0.13	88.23
BCC Carnia e Gemonese	10	2	12	0	6	6	0	0	0	12	0.13	88.36
BCC Santo Stefano Martellago	0	12	10	2	9	2	0	0	1	12	0.13	88.49
BCC Sesto San Giovanni	0	12	11	1	12	0	0	0	0	12	0.13	88.62
Banca del Fucino	0	12	8	4	6	5	0	1	0	12	0.13	88.76
Banco di Lucca e del Tirreno	1	11	11	1	12	0	0	0	0	12	0.13	88.89
CRA Roana BCC	0	12	11	1	10	1	0	1	0	12	0.13	89.02
CRU Bassa Vallagarina	0	12	12	0	8	4	0	0	0	12	0.13	89.15
CRU Rabbi e Caldes	0	12	12	0	4	0	0	6	2	12	0.13	89.28
CRU Valsugana e Tesino	0	12	12	0	5	5	0	1	1	12	0.13	89.41
BCC Gradara	0	11	11	0	11	0	0	0	0	11	0.12	89.53
BCC Padovana	0	11	9	2	3	0	0	8	0	11	0.12	89.65
BCC San Giovanni Rotondo	0	11	11	0	9	2	0	0	0	11	0.12	89.77
BCC Valdarno Fiorentino	8	3	11	0	11	0	0	0	0	11	0.12	89.89
BCC Valpolicella Benaco Banca	0	11	11	0	8	0	0	3	0	11	0.12	90.01

(continued)

Table A2 (continued)

	Listing		Seniority		Return					Total		
	Listed	Unlisted	Senior	Subordinated	Fixed rate	Fixed rate + variable	Fixed rate + Zero Coupon	Variable rate	Zero Coupon	Freq.	%	Cumul. (%)
BCCCastelli Romani e Tuscolo	9	2	11	0	11	0	0	0	0	11	0.12	90.13
Banca Popolare Frusinate	0	11	11	0	10	1	0	0	0	11	0.12	90.25
Banca Romagna Centro e Macerone Credi..	2	9	8	3	5	0	0	3	3	11	0.12	90.37
CRA Treviso	0	11	11	0	10	1	0	0	0	11	0.12	90.49
CRU Selva di Val Gardena	0	11	11	0	7	1	0	3	0	11	0.12	90.61
Dexia Crediop	9	2	11	0	2	5	2	0	2	11	0.12	90.73
BCC Centro Lazio	0	10	10	0	10	0	0	0	0	10	0.11	90.84
BCC Don Rizzo	0	10	10	0	10	0	0	0	0	10	0.11	90.95
BCC Gatteo	1	9	6	4	6	2	0	2	0	10	0.11	91.06
BCC Sant'Andrea di Suasa	0	10	10	0	10	0	0	0	0	10	0.11	91.17
BCC Trevigiano	0	10	10	0	5	0	0	2	3	10	0.11	91.28
BCC Verolavecchia	9	1	10	0	9	0	0	0	1	10	0.11	91.39
Banca Interprovinciale	0	10	10	0	10	0	0	0	0	10	0.11	91.50
Banca Popolare di Mantova	0	10	10	0	9	1	0	0	0	10	0.11	91.60
Banca Reale	0	10	10	0	7	2	0	1	0	10	0.11	91.71
CRA Borgo San Giacomo	0	10	10	0	10	0	0	0	0	10	0.11	91.82
CRU Trento	0	10	10	0	8	0	0	0	2	10	0.11	91.93
IBL Istituto Bancario del Lavoro	0	10	0	10	6	0	0	4	0	10	0.11	92.04
BCC Agro Pontino	5	4	9	0	9	0	0	0	0	9	0.10	92.14
BCC Bassa Friulana	0	9	9	0	6	0	0	3	0	9	0.10	92.24
BCC Civitanova Marche	0	9	9	0	8	1	0	0	0	9	0.10	92.34
BCC Flumeri	0	9	9	0	9	0	0	0	0	9	0.10	92.43
BCC Giuseppe Toniolo di Genzano	6	3	9	0	9	0	0	0	0	9	0.10	92.53
BCC La Riscossa di Regalbuto	0	9	9	0	9	0	0	0	0	9	0.10	92.63
BCC Lesmo	0	9	9	0	9	0	0	0	0	9	0.10	92.73

(continued)

Table A2 (continued)

	Listing		Seniority		Return					Total		
	Listed	Unlisted	Senior	Subordinated	Fixed rate	Fixed rate + variable	Fixed rate + Zero Coupon	Variable rate	Zero Coupon	Freq.	%	Cumul. (%)
BCC Mugello	9	0	9	0	6	0	0	3	0	9	0.10	92.83
BCC Nettuno	8	1	9	0	9	0	0	0	0	9	0.10	92.93
BCC Reggiano	0	9	9	0	4	5	0	0	0	9	0.10	93.02
BCC Valsassina	6	3	9	0	9	0	0	0	0	9	0.10	93.12
Banca Liquidazione coatta	0	9	0	9	7	0	0	2	0	9	0.10	93.22
Banca Popolare di Sviluppo	0	9	9	0	7	0	0	2	0	9	0.10	93.32
BCC Borghetto Lodigiano	0	8	8	0	8	0	0	0	0	8	0.09	93.41
BCC Carso	0	8	8	0	6	0	0	2	0	8	0.09	93.49
BCC Isera	0	8	8	0	1	2	0	3	2	8	0.09	93.58
BCC Ledro	0	8	8	0	3	0	0	1	4	8	0.09	93.67
BCC Lizzana	0	8	8	0	4	0	0	2	2	8	0.09	93.76
BCC Mantignana	0	8	8	0	7	1	0	0	0	8	0.09	93.84
BCC Spello e Bettona	0	8	7	1	6	0	0	0	2	8	0.09	93.93
BCC Veneziano	0	8	6	2	2	0	0	5	1	8	0.09	94.02
CR Pinetana Fornace e Seregnano	0	8	8	0	8	0	0	0	0	8	0.09	94.10
CRA BCC di Battipaglia e Montecorvino..	0	8	8	0	8	0	0	0	0	8	0.09	94.19
CRA Paliano	7	1	8	0	8	0	0	0	0	8	0.09	94.28
CRU Rovere' Della Luna	0	8	8	0	6	0	0	0	2	8	0.09	94.37
Credito di Romagna	0	8	2	6	6	1	0	1	0	8	0.09	94.45
BCC Annia di Cartura e Polesine	0	7	7	0	1	6	0	0	0	7	0.08	94.53
BCC Montepaone	2	5	6	1	7	0	0	0	0	7	0.08	94.61
BCC Pesaro	0	7	7	0	6	1	0	0	0	7	0.08	94.68
BCC Pratola Peligna	7	0	7	0	6	0	0	1	0	7	0.08	94.76
BCC Tassullo e Nanno	0	7	7	0	4	0	0	1	2	7	0.08	94.84
BCC Valmarecchia	0	7	7	0	3	2	0	1	1	7	0.08	94.91
BCC Viterbo	0	7	7	0	5	0	0	2	0	7	0.08	94.99
Banca Intermobiliare	4	3	7	0	4	2	0	1	0	7	0.08	95.07
CR Levico Terme	0	7	7	0	5	0	0	2	0	7	0.08	95.14
CRU Prato Allo Stelvio	0	7	7	0	4	0	0	3	0	7	0.08	95.22

(continued)

Table A2 (continued)

	Listing		Seniority		Return					Total		
	Listed	Unlisted	Senior	Subordinated	Fixed rate	Fixed rate + variable	Fixed rate + Zero Coupon	Variable rate	Zero Coupon	Freq.	%	Cumul. (%)
Cassa Risparmio Orvieto	0	7	7	0	7	0	0	0	0	7	0.08	95.29
Credito Lombardo Veneto	0	7	7	0	7	0	0	0	0	7	0.08	95.37
BCC Banco Fiorentino	4	2	6	0	1	5	0	0	0	6	0.07	95.44
BCC Doberdo' e Savogna	6	0	6	0	4	1	0	1	0	6	0.07	95.50
BCC Dovera e Postino	5	1	6	0	4	0	0	2	0	6	0.07	95.57
BCC Formello	3	3	6	0	4	1	0	1	0	6	0.07	95.63
BCC Monteriggioni	4	2	6	0	0	0	0	0	6	6	0.07	95.70
BCC Mozzanica	3	3	6	0	6	0	0	0	0	6	0.07	95.76
BCC Ostra Vetere	0	6	6	0	6	0	0	0	0	6	0.07	95.83
BCC Sassano	0	6	6	0	5	1	0	0	0	6	0.07	95.90
Banca Bovio Calderari	0	6	2	4	2	0	0	4	0	6	0.07	95.96
Banca Esperia	0	6	6	0	2	0	0	4	0	6	0.07	96.03
Banca Popolare Valconca	0	6	6	0	0	0	0	6	0	6	0.07	96.09
Banca Popolare di Cassinate	0	6	6	0	6	0	0	0	0	6	0.07	96.16
Banca Popolare di Cortona	0	6	6	0	6	0	0	0	0	6	0.07	96.22
Banca di Cividale	1	5	4	2	1	2	0	3	0	6	0.07	96.29
CRU Folgaria	0	6	3	3	3	0	0	0	3	6	0.07	96.35
Cassa Raiffeisen Oltradige	0	6	6	0	4	1	0	1	0	6	0.07	96.42
BCC Abruzzese Cappelle sul Tavo	4	1	5	0	5	0	0	0	0	5	0.05	96.47
BCC Alto Reno	0	5	5	0	5	0	0	0	0	5	0.05	96.53
BCC Anagni	0	5	5	0	5	0	0	0	0	5	0.05	96.58
BCC Bancasciano	3	2	3	2	5	0	0	0	0	5	0.05	96.64
BCC Cagliari	0	5	5	0	5	0	0	0	0	5	0.05	96.69
BCC Cesena e Ronta	0	5	5	0	0	0	0	4	1	5	0.05	96.75
BCC Polesine Villadose	0	5	3	2	3	1	0	0	1	5	0.05	96.80
BCC Ronciglione	0	5	5	0	5	0	0	0	0	5	0.05	96.86
BCC Vergato	0	5	5	0	3	0	0	2	0	5	0.05	96.91
BCC Vestenanova	0	5	5	0	5	0	0	0	0	5	0.05	96.97

(continued)

Table A2 (continued)

	Listing		Seniority		Return					Total		
	Listed	Unlisted	Senior	Subordinated	Fixed rate	Fixed rate + variable	Fixed rate + Zero Coupon	Variable rate	Zero Coupon	Freq.	%	Cumul. (%)
Banca Galileo	0	5	5	0	1	2	0	2	0	5	0.05	97.02
Banca Passadore	0	5	5	0	0	0	0	5	0	5	0.05	97.07
Banca Popolare Etruria Lazio(ex)	0	5	0	5	3	0	0	2	0	5	0.05	97.13
Banca di Credito Cooperativo del Vibo..	3	2	5	0	4	1	0	0	0	5	0.05	97.18
CR Saone	0	5	5	0	5	0	0	0	0	5	0.05	97.24
CRU Don Lorenzo Guetti	0	5	5	0	5	0	0	0	0	5	0.05	97.29
Mediocredito Centrale	4	1	5	0	0	1	2	1	1	5	0.05	97.35
BCC Agrigentino	4	0	2	2	4	0	0	0	0	4	0.04	97.39
BCC Alberobello	0	4	4	0	4	0	0	0	0	4	0.04	97.43
BCC Antonello da Messina	4	0	0	4	3	0	0	1	0	4	0.04	97.48
BCC Avetrana	0	4	4	0	3	1	0	0	0	4	0.04	97.52
BCC Barbarano Romano	4	0	4	0	4	0	0	0	0	4	0.04	97.57
BCC Barlassina	0	4	4	0	4	0	0	0	0	4	0.04	97.61
BCC Camerano	0	4	3	1	4	0	0	0	0	4	0.04	97.65
BCC Cassano Murge	0	4	4	0	4	0	0	0	0	4	0.04	97.70
BCC Circeo	3	1	4	0	4	0	0	0	0	4	0.04	97.74
BCC Lezzeno	4	0	4	0	4	0	0	0	0	4	0.04	97.78
BCC Monterenzio	0	4	4	0	3	0	0	1	0	4	0.04	97.83
BCC Velino	4	0	4	0	4	0	0	0	0	4	0.04	97.87
Banca Sistema	0	4	1	3	1	1	0	2	0	4	0.04	97.91
Banca del Monte di Lucca	0	4	3	1	1	0	0	3	0	4	0.04	97.96
Banca del Vecchio	0	4	4	0	3	0	0	0	1	4	0.04	98.00
Banca delle Marche (ex)	0	4	0	4	4	0	0	0	0	4	0.04	98.05
Banca di Credito Cooperativo di Napoli	0	4	4	0	4	0	0	0	0	4	0.04	98.09
CR Mezzolombardo e S Michele A/A	0	4	4	0	2	0	0	0	2	4	0.04	98.13
CRU Alta Vallagarina	0	4	4	0	0	0	0	0	4	4	0.04	98.18
Cassa Risparmio Fermo	0	4	4	0	4	0	0	0	0	4	0.04	98.22
Cassa Risparmio Teramo	0	4	4	0	2	0	0	0	2	4	0.04	98.26

(continued)

Table A2 (continued)

	Listing		Seniority		Return					Total		
	Listed	Unlisted	Senior	Subordinated	Fixed rate	Fixed rate + variable	Fixed rate + Zero Coupon	Variable rate	Zero Coupon	Freq.	%	Cumul. (%)
Cerea	0	4	4	0	4	0	0	0	0	4	0.04	98.31
FarBanca	0	4	4	0	0	0	0	4	0	4	0.04	98.35
Mediocredito Friuli	1	3	4	0	1	1	0	2	0	4	0.04	98.40
Mediocredito Trentino A.A.	0	4	4	0	3	0	0	1	0	4	0.04	98.44
BCC Buonabitacolo	0	3	3	0	3	0	0	0	0	3	0.03	98.47
BCC Centro Calabria	0	3	2	1	3	0	0	0	0	3	0.03	98.50
BCC Comuni Cilentani	0	3	3	0	1	1	0	1	0	3	0.03	98.54
BCC Gambatesa	0	3	3	0	3	0	0	0	0	3	0.03	98.57
BCC Orobica	0	3	3	0	3	0	0	0	0	3	0.03	98.60
BCC Padana Orientale Rovigo	0	3	2	1	3	0	0	0	0	3	0.03	98.64
BCC San Marco dei Cavoti	0	3	3	0	3	0	0	0	0	3	0.03	98.67
BCC Sangro Teatina	3	0	3	0	3	0	0	0	0	3	0.03	98.70
BCC Santeramo in Colle	0	3	3	0	3	0	0	0	0	3	0.03	98.73
Banca del Cilento	0	3	2	1	2	0	0	0	1	3	0.03	98.77
Bancassurance Popolari	2	1	0	3	3	0	0	0	0	3	0.03	98.80
CCB Nord Est	0	3	2	1	1	0	0	0	2	3	0.03	98.83
CRU Valle Isarco	0	3	3	0	3	0	0	0	0	3	0.03	98.86
Cassa Risparmio Chieti (ex)	0	3	0	3	2	0	0	1	0	3	0.03	98.90
Credito Salernitano	0	3	0	3	3	0	0	0	0	3	0.03	98.93
Prader Bank	0	3	3	0	0	0	0	3	0	3	0.03	98.96
BCC Adige Po Lusia	0	2	0	2	1	1	0	0	0	2	0.02	98.98
BCC Adria del Delta	0	2	2	0	1	0	0	0	1	2	0.02	99.01
BCC Bellegra	2	0	2	0	2	0	0	0	0	2	0.02	99.03
BCC Brutia	1	1	0	2	2	0	0	0	0	2	0.02	99.05
BCC Creta di Castelsangiovanni	0	2	1	1	2	0	0	0	0	2	0.02	99.07
BCC Euganea	1	1	1	1	2	0	0	0	0	2	0.02	99.09
BCC Gaudiano di Lavello	0	2	0	2	2	0	0	0	0	2	0.02	99.12
BCC Pietro Grammatico di Paceco	2	0	2	0	2	0	0	0	0	2	0.02	99.14
BCC Ripatransone	0	2	2	0	2	0	0	0	0	2	0.02	99.16
BCC San Barnaba di Marino	2	0	2	0	2	0	0	0	0	2	0.02	99.18

(continued)

Table A2 (continued)

	Listing		Seniority		Return					Total		
	Listed	Unlisted	Senior	Subordinated	Fixed rate	Fixed rate + variable	Fixed rate + Zero Coupon	Variable rate	Zero Coupon	Freq.	%	Cumul. (%)
BCC San Michele di Caltanissetta	2	0	2	0	2	0	0	0	0	2	0.02	99.20
BCR di Romagna	0	2	2	0	2	0	0	0	0	2	0.02	99.22
Banca Farmafactoring	2	0	2	0	1	1	0	0	0	2	0.02	99.25
Banca Italease	0	2	2	0	0	1	0	1	0	2	0.02	99.27
Banca Promos	0	2	2	0	2	0	0	0	0	2	0.02	99.29
CR Centrofiemme Cavalese	0	2	2	0	2	0	0	0	0	2	0.02	99.31
CRU Centro Valsugana	0	2	2	0	0	0	0	0	2	2	0.02	99.33
CRU Strembo Bocenago e Caderzone	0	2	2	0	1	0	0	0	1	2	0.02	99.36
CRU Valle dei Laghi	0	2	1	1	2	0	0	0	0	2	0.02	99.38
Cassa Rurale Altipiani BCC	0	2	0	2	2	0	0	0	0	2	0.02	99.40
Deutsche Bank SpA	1	1	1	1	1	0	0	1	0	2	0.02	99.42
Imprebanca	0	2	2	0	1	0	0	1	0	2	0.02	99.44
Interbanca	2	0	2	0	0	1	1	0	0	2	0.02	99.47
Quadra Fiave' B.C.C.	0	2	2	0	0	0	0	0	2	2	0.02	99.49
Alto Tirreno Della Calabria Verbicaro	1	0	0	1	1	0	0	0	0	1	0.01	99.50
BCC Alta Murgia	0	1	1	0	1	0	0	0	0	1	0.01	99.51
BCC Alta Padovana	0	1	1	0	1	0	0	0	0	1	0.01	99.52
BCC Apuana	1	0	1	0	0	0	0	0	1	1	0.01	99.53
BCC Basciano	1	0	1	0	0	0	0	1	0	1	0.01	99.54
BCC Bolognese	0	1	1	0	0	0	0	1	0	1	0.01	99.55
BCC Capranica e Bassano Romano	0	1	0	1	0	0	0	1	0	1	0.01	99.56
BCC Falconara Marittima	0	1	1	0	1	0	0	0	0	1	0.01	99.57
BCC Fermano	0	1	0	1	0	0	0	1	0	1	0.01	99.59
BCC Parma	0	1	0	1	1	0	0	0	0	1	0.01	99.60
BCC Polesine Rovigo	0	1	0	1	1	0	0	0	0	1	0.01	99.61
BCC Putignano	0	1	0	1	1	0	0	0	0	1	0.01	99.62
BCC Recanati e Colmurano	0	1	0	1	1	0	0	0	0	1	0.01	99.63

(continued)

Table A2 (continued)

	Listing		Seniority		Return					Total		
	Listed	Unlisted	Senior	Subordinated	Fixed rate	Fixed rate + variable	Fixed rate + Zero Coupon	Variable rate	Zero Coupon	Freq.	%	Cumul. (%)
BCC Rivarolo Canavese e Rivara	0	1	0	1	1	0	0	0	0	1	0.01	99.64
BCC San Vincenzo De' Paoli	0	1	1	0	1	0	0	0	0	1	0.01	99.65
BCC Taranto	0	1	1	0	1	0	0	0	0	1	0.01	99.66
BCC Tuscia	0	1	0	1	0	0	0	1	0	1	0.01	99.67
BCC Valledolmo	1	0	1	0	1	0	0	0	0	1	0.01	99.68
BCC Vigevano	0	1	0	1	1	0	0	0	0	1	0.01	99.69
BCC del Vomano	0	1	0	1	1	0	0	0	0	1	0.01	99.71
Banca IFIS	1	0	1	0	1	0	0	0	0	1	0.01	99.72
Banca Lavoro e Risparmio	0	1	1	0	1	0	0	0	0	1	0.01	99.73
Banca Leonardo	1	0	1	0	0	1	0	0	0	1	0.01	99.74
Banca Meridiana	0	1	0	1	0	0	0	1	0	1	0.01	99.75
Banca Popolare del Mediterraneo	0	1	0	1	1	0	0	0	0	1	0.01	99.76
Banca Popolare di Marostica	0	1	1	0	1	0	0	0	0	1	0.01	99.77
Banca Progetto	0	1	1	0	1	0	0	0	0	1	0.01	99.78
Banca Santa Giulia	0	1	1	0	0	0	0	1	0	1	0.01	99.79
Banca Verde	0	1	1	0	0	0	0	0	1	1	0.01	99.80
Banca di Bergamo	0	1	0	1	0	0	0	1	0	1	0.01	99.81
Banca di Macerata	0	1	1	0	1	0	0	0	0	1	0.01	99.83
Banco Emiliano BCC	0	1	1	0	1	0	0	0	0	1	0.01	99.84
CRU Bassa Atesina	0	1	1	0	0	0	0	1	0	1	0.01	99.85
CRU Bassa Valsugana	0	1	1	0	1	0	0	0	0	1	0.01	99.86
CRU Naturno	0	1	1	0	1	0	0	0	0	1	0.01	99.87
Cassa Risparmio Pescara	0	1	1	0	1	0	0	0	0	1	0.01	99.88
Cassa Rurale Val Rendena	0	1	1	0	1	0	0	0	0	1	0.01	99.89
ExtraBanca	0	1	1	0	1	0	0	0	0	1	0.01	99.90
Finnat Euramerica	0	1	1	0	0	0	0	1	0	1	0.01	99.91

(continued)

Table A2 (continued)

	Listing		Seniority		Return					Total		
	Listed	Unlisted	Senior	Subordinated	Fixed rate	Fixed rate + variable	Fixed rate + Zero Coupon	Variable rate	Zero Coupon	Freq.	%	Cumul. (%)
GBM Gruppo Bancario Mediterraneo	0	1	1	0	1	0	0	0	0	1	0.01	99.92
IW Bank	0	1	0	1	0	0	0	1	0	1	0.01	99.93
Invest Banca	0	1	0	1	1	0	0	0	0	1	0.01	99.95
Mediocredito CentroItalia	0	1	1	0	1	0	0	0	0	1	0.01	99.96
Mediocredito Italiano	0	1	1	0	0	0	0	1	0	1	0.01	99.97
Nord Est Banca	0	1	1	0	0	1	0	0	0	1	0.01	99.98
Spiazzo B.C.C.	0	1	1	0	0	0	0	0	1	1	0.01	99.99
Tione Ragoli e Montagne B.C.C.	0	1	1	0	0	0	0	0	1	1	0.01	100.00
Total	**2,189**	**6,971**	**8,517**	**643**	**6,197**	**949**	**11**	**1,607**	**396**	**9,160**	**100**	

References

ABI, 2017. Monthly Outlook. Economia e Mercati Finanziari-Creditizi. Roma, July.

Beau, E., Hill, J., Hussain, T., Nixon, D., 2014. Bank funding costs: What are they, what determines them and why do they matter? Bank of England, Quarterly Bulletin.

Bianchi, M.L., 2014. An analysis on the difference between bank index-linked bonds' prices and their fair-value. Bancaria 6, 28–48.

Canestri, D., Amadei, L., 2001. Reverse Convertible: Costruzione e analisi degli effetti sul mercato dei titoli sottostanti. Quaderni di Finanza No. 48, Consob.

Carlando, L., 2012. L'offerta al pubblico di obbligazioni bancarie: la disciplina del prospetto alla luce delle ultime modifiche al Regolamento Emittenti. Diritto Bancario, Rivista, 1–22.

Consob, 2011. Raccolta bancaria a mezzo di obbligazioni, prospetto e regole di condotto. Documento di consultazione, 13 Luglio.

Dell'Aversano, F., Lopes, A., 2014. Il sistema bancario italiano tra efficienza e stabilità ai tempi della crisi. IPE Working Paper No. 2.

Gabbi, G., Sironi, A., 2005. Which factors affect corporate bonds pricing? Empirical evidence from eurobonds primary market spreads. The European Journal of Finance 11 (1), 59–74.

F. Crespi and D. V. Mascia, *Bank Funding Strategies*, Palgrave Macmillan Studies in Banking and Financial Institutions, https://doi.org/10.1007/978-3-319-69413-9

Iannotta, G., 2011. Market discipline in the banking industry: Evidence from spread dispersion. The European Journal of Finance 17 (2), 111–131.

Lopez, J.A., Spiegel, M., 2014. International Evidence on Bank Funding Profiles and Performance: Are Banks "Overbanked"? Unpublished manuscript.

Mascia, D.V., Mattana, P., Rossi, S.P.S., D'Aietti, R., 2016. Sovereign and bank CDS spreads during the European Debt Crisis: Laying the foundation for SMEs' financial distress—in Rossi, S.P.S. (Ed.), "Access to Bank Credit and SME Financing", Palgrave Macmillan Studies in Banking and Financial Institutions Series, London.

SRB, 2016. The single resolution mechanism. Introduction to resolution planning. Publications Office of the European Union, Luxembourg.

Zoli, E., 2013. Italian sovereign spreads: Their determinants and pass-through to bank funding costs and lending conditions. IMF WP/13/84.

Index

A

Asset and liability management 3

B

Bail-in 3, 94–102, 104, 109, 111–113, 117
Bail-inable 14, 15, 99
Bail-inable instruments 100, 108, 113
Bail-out 94–96, 100, 106, 109–111, 117
Banca delle Marche 109
Banca Popolare dell'Etruria e del Lazio 109, 110
Banca Popolare di Vicenza 111, 112
Bank of Italy 52, 55, 56, 58–62, 71, 72, 94, 100, 103, 108, 109
Bank Recovery and Resolution Directive (BRRD) 3, 14, 94–96, 98–100, 102, 104, 106, 108–110, 112–114, 118
Bond 3–5, 7, 12, 16, 20, 26, 28, 33, 46, 50–52, 56–66, 70–77, 79–86, 89–91, 95, 100–104, 106–110, 114, 117, 118

C

Capital injection 57, 110, 112
Cassa di Risparmio della Provincia di Chieti 109
Cassa di Risparmio di Ferrara 109
Commercial Paper 5
Common Equity Tier 1 (CET1) 57, 99
Consob 71–74, 76, 79, 80, 110
Convertibles bonds 71
Covered bond 16, 17, 20, 83, 84, 98
Credit linked notes 70, 77, 79, 81, 84, 85
Currency linked 64, 81, 84, 85

F. Crespi and D. V. Mascia, *Bank Funding Strategies*, Palgrave Macmillan Studies in Banking and Financial Institutions, https://doi.org/10.1007/978-3-319-69413-9

D

Debt securities 18–22, 26, 28, 29, 31, 33, 34, 36, 65, 71, 91
Deposit 2, 3, 5–7, 10, 11, 15–22, 26, 28, 29, 33, 36, 39, 43, 46, 50–52, 54–60, 62, 66, 76, 98–100, 108, 117, 118
Deposit guarantee scheme 14, 96, 99, 109

E

Equity 2, 3, 5, 9, 10, 13, 14, 50, 51, 57, 58, 62, 73, 81, 84, 85, 94, 98, 99, 109
Equity linked bonds 70
Euro area crisis 15, 20, 51, 56
Euro area debt crisis 29, 96
European Central Bank (ECB) 4, 15–18, 20–23, 27, 28, 30, 31, 34, 36, 37, 39, 41, 43, 44, 46, 52, 57, 94, 97, 103, 107
European Deposit Insurance Scheme (EDIS) 98

F

Failing or likely to fail (FOLTF) 111
Financial crises 4, 6, 8, 11, 15, 16, 18–21, 25, 26, 43, 46, 51, 54, 56, 94, 95, 107–109, 113, 117
Financial wealth 51, 52, 62
Fixed 3, 9, 28, 29, 66, 73, 75, 77, 81, 82, 84–90, 102
Floating 81, 82, 84–86, 102
Funding 2–7, 10, 11, 13, 15–29, 33, 39, 46, 50, 51, 54, 56–58, 60, 61, 63, 70, 83, 90, 95, 98–103, 106, 114, 117, 118
Funding strategies 3, 4, 7, 8, 10–12, 15, 18, 19, 22–24, 27, 46, 50–52, 65, 66, 103, 117
Funding structures 4, 23, 27, 56
Fund linked 81, 84, 85

G

Global Systemically Important Banks (G-SIB) 14

H

Households 5, 6, 50–54, 57, 61–66, 70, 83, 90, 108

I

Index linked 81, 83–86
Inflation linked 70, 74, 75, 81, 83–86, 88
Insurance Distribution Directive (IDD) 7
Interest rate linked 81, 84–86

L

Liability management 3, 4
Liquidation 99, 111, 112, 114
Liquidity Coverage Ratio (LCR) 11, 12
Listed bonds 79
Loans 2–5, 11, 17, 27–29, 43, 44, 46, 54, 57–60, 103, 106–108, 117
Long-Term Refinancing Operations (LTROs) 17, 22

M

MIFID 7, 62, 63, 67, 71, 72, 74, 76, 113
Minimum Requirement for own funds and Eligible Liabilities (MREL) 14
Monte dei Paschi di Siena 51, 87, 101, 112

N

Net Stable Funding Ratio (NSFR) 3, 12, 13, 26

P

Perpetual preferred securities 81
Plain vanilla 65, 66, 76, 77, 80, 82–84, 86, 89, 90, 118
Precautionary recapitalization 112, 114

R

Recapitalization 14, 57, 95, 110
Redeemable bond 81, 84, 85
Resolution 14, 83, 94–99, 106, 109, 110, 112, 114
Resolution authority 14, 94, 97–100, 109, 118
Resolution tools 96, 99
Retail investors 4, 62, 65, 66, 70–72, 74, 76, 79, 83, 86, 87, 90, 91, 100, 104, 107–111, 118

S

Senior bonds 82, 84
Single Resolution Board (SRB) 98, 111
Single Resolution Fund (SRF) 98
Single Resolution Mechanism (SRM) 97, 98
Single Supervisory Mechanism (SSM) 53, 97
Sovereign debt crisis 52, 57, 97, 108
Structured products 65, 76, 77, 79
Subordinated bonds 65, 77, 83, 84, 108, 110, 118

T

Total Loss-Absorbing Capacity (TLAC) 3, 14

U

Unlisted bonds 83, 101, 102

V

Veneto Banca 101, 111, 112

W

Wholesale funding 2, 3, 5–8, 17–20, 25, 46, 56, 117

Z

Zero coupon bond 82

The manufacturer's authorised representative in the EU is Springer Nature Customer Service Centre GmbH, Europaplatz 3, 69115 Heidelberg, Germany. If you have any concerns regarding our products, please contact ProductSafety@springernature.com

Printed and bound by CPI Group (UK) Ltd, Croydon, CR0 4YY
22/09/2026
02221070-0006